D0915539

A CIRCULAR JOURNEY

Rome Burning, poetry
Umbertina, a novel
The Dream Book: An Anthology of Writings by Italian American Women
Love in the Middle Ages, a novel
More Italian Hours, short fiction
Festa: Recipes & Recollections of Italian Holidays
Aldus and His Dream Book
Chiaroscuro: Essays of Identity

A CIRCULAR JOURNEY

Helen Barolini

Fordham University Press NEW YORK 2006

Library of Congress Cataloging-in-Publication Data

Barolini, Helen, 1925–
   A circular journey / by Helen Barolini.
     p. cm.
   ISBN-13: 978-0-8232-2615-3 (hardcover : alk. paper)
   ISBN-10: 0-8232-2615-8 (hardcover : alk. paper)
   I. Barolini, Helen, 1925–   2. Authors, American—20th century—
Biography.   3. Italian American women—Intellectual life.   4. American
literature—Italian influences.   5. Italian Americans in literature.   I. Title.

   PS3552.A725Z46   2006
   818'.5409—dc22

                       2006007964

These essays originally appeared in the following publications: "A Classical Excursion" and "Sicily, Light and Dark," *Kenyon Review*; "The Spinsters of Taos," *Prairie Schooner*; "Neruda vs. Sartre," *Paris Review*; "A Circular Journey," *Texas Quarterly*; "Souvenirs of Venice," "My Mother's Wedding Day," "Shutting the Door on Someone," and "Montale and Mosca in a Train," *Southwest Review*; "Paris in the Boondocks," *Antioch Review*; "Zio Filippo at Summer Camp," *New Letters*; "A Fish Tale," *Missouri Review*.

Printed in the United States of America
08 07 06 5 4 3 2 1
First edition.

For Frank Gado, *amico a tutta prova*

. . . every end is a beginning. . . . life . . . is a self-evolving circle, which, from a ring imperceptibly small, rushes on all sides outwards to new and larger circles, and that without end.

—Ralph Waldo Emerson

CONTENTS

I Home

2004 James Street

James Street, where I lived from infancy through my twenty-second year, begins in downtown Syracuse at Clinton Square, continues a straight course eastbound reaching an elevated point at Oak Street, then proceeds on to become a commercial artery in the Eastwood neighborhood, ending miles from start in East Syracuse. The James Street I knew was the city's grandest residential thoroughfare, flanked in its lower numbered blocks by full-growth, stately trees and mansions in a range of opulent architectural styles. One visitor of the last century called it "the 5th Avenue of Syracuse," one of the handsomest American streets he had ever seen. By the 1000 block the look gradually morphs into handsome but less grand homes, and finally into more modest dwellings in its eastern stretch. It is by chance (but Freud says there are no accidents) that in the year 2004 my thoughts go back over the decades to fix on the two-family house at 2004 James Street where my conscious life began.

I once walked James Street in both directions—first as a schoolgirl toward Eastwood for Saturday confession and Sunday School at the Blessed Sacrament Church, stopping along the way to collect chestnut burrs or autumn leaves for waxing, or hopping squeamishly over earthworms on the sidewalk in spring, then stomping on summer's white berries from a snowberry bush to hear the explosive pop they made. Later, a graduate of Syracuse University, I went in the opposite direction toward downtown for my first job as an advertising copywriter in the E. W. Edwards

3

department store. With my lunch in a bag I walked to work and back, saving bus fare, for I was filled with dreams of other cities—London! Paris! Rome! And what fed those dreams was not only literature but also the sight of the stately James Street homes and grounds I passed, inspired I imagined by the European travels of their owners.

Near the beginning of James Street, at the corner with State Street, had stood the former Lynch mansion still elegant as Syracuse's Fine Arts Museum. But it was razed in 1968 and the site is now occupied by a gas station while the collection, renamed the Everson Museum, is housed in a bland new edifice opposite the Oncenter Complex of buildings that includes the War Memorial sports arena, a Convention Center, three Civic Center Theaters, and a huge parking garage. More always seems to trump fine in my old hometown.

James Street in its prime is now only memory as I recall there the red stone Italianate residence that became the Goodyear-Burlingame private school and was, for the short time his family resided in Syracuse, attended by a very young F. Scott Fitzgerald. In a piece I wrote about my father called "The Way of the World," I juxtaposed him with Fitzgerald, with whom he shared a birth year and early Syracuse childhood. The old Goodyear school is gone now, as is romantic Sedgwick Cottage, a Gothic Revival home rich with architectural detailing and matching stables at 742 James, designed in 1845 by the noted architect Alexander Jackson Davis—a distinction that did not save that treasure from demolition.

Farther on, behind ornate wrought iron gates at 918 James Street, there once rose the turrets of "Uarda" the mysteriously named grey stone castle of Flora B. Smith, heiress to the L. C. Smith typewriter fortune. Opposite stood the stately pale gray, white-columned residence of Episcopal Bishop Peabody and the plantation-style mansion of the department store Edwards family with its gigantic columned portico. Just past Oak Street, the last of the mansions, an enchanting French chateau, was bulldozed to give way to a motel. Now should I walk past I'd no longer view the lush grounds of former days but perhaps salesmen at breakfast in the glassed-in coffee shop facing the street.

"Next to Go" run the photo captions of the 1950s in the *Post-Standard* showing one landmark after another marked for demolition after the fall of Flora B. Smith's castle. "Nob Hill No Longer" ran a *Herald-Journal* headline. Even the great trees were gone, victims of the Dutch elm disease that decimated them though I've never understood why the State College of Forestry, located at Syracuse University, could not have done something preventive. Alone surviving intact the downfall of James Street was Judge Hiscock's Palladian mansion that, after his death, became The Corinthian Club, an upscale woman's club. Otherwise, my birthplace has been unrelenting in tearing down its most architecturally important landmarks and replacing them with insignificant commercial properties or parking lots. That urge to tear down must have been there in 1868 when Charles Dickens was in town for a reading and said the place looked as if it had begun to be built yesterday.

Now Syracuse's downtown has gone the way of many American cities and seen its center dwindle as businesses and shops decamped to the malls. Shorn of its grand Hotel Onondaga once known as upstate New York's finest, its several department stores and then even the original Schrafft's of that once popular chain of restaurants, as well as the palatial movie theaters of other times with their plush interiors of loges and balconies, mighty organs, chandeliers, painted scenic views above the stage, and imposing gold-fringed curtains that were drawn when the film began, downtown had become for me a wasteland. "That's progress," my father, an unflinching pragmatist, would always say as old-time pleasures and amenities disappeared. His was total acceptance of

5

the city fathers' philosophy, an abiding belief in growth with no thought for preservation. If that view ever fit the times and place, it has but a questionable future. For when growth halts and decline sets in, what then? The thriving city I grew up in had a population of 250,000 and was the fourth largest city in the state. No longer—in 2000 Syracuse's population was 147,000 and was topped by Yonkers as fourth in the state.

My father had overcome his own losses at the old Regional market when his produce company burned down and he moved to a new location where his business thrived so that he became ever more convinced that the old should give way to the new. But even in his time there was no more edible pike to be fished from a polluted Oneida Lake, site of the Syracuse Yacht and Country Club where he golfed and had once relished Oneida Lake pike in the club dining room, bragging of it to his guests.

About midway on James Street was the hillside residence of one of the city's captains of industry and his large family which included two sets of twin daughters around my age. When I was in high school all the twins were away at "Dobbs" as the Miss Masters' boarding school at Dobbs Ferry on the Hudson was known. I absorbed the family's importance from my mother who kept abreast of status through the social pages of the local papers. So, when during World War II the two sets of twins and I happened to participate in the same summer vacation training course for nurses' aides that was part of the war effort to alleviate the shortage of nurses in hospitals, I was properly impressed. That was the war we all believed in and in which we all participated with victory gardens, ration coupons, volunteer work, war bonds. I don't recall that the twins and I ever exchanged words, I was simply aware of them as I was aware of all gradation in status. Family status was visible as the houses on James Street gradually got smaller and less individualized until finally, on the corner of Peck Ave and James Street, the presence of Galloway's corner

Drug Store with its window display "Be Happy!—Go Lucky" for Lucky Strike cigarettes, and an adjoining grocery signaled that greater James Street had passed from elite to notable to ordinary.

We lived diagonally across the street from Galloway's in a yellow two-family house on a block of two-families. Then came Eastwood, once a separate village, but incorporated into expanding Syracuse in 1895. Was it, I wonder now, named for that Eastwood in England where D. H. Lawrence happened to be born? Our Eastwood had many attractions—a Woolworth's 5- and 10-cent store, the Palace movie theater, a branch library, the James bakery in its Art Deco building, inexpensive dress and sundry shops where I could buy $1.00 gifts for Mother's Day, a Marble Farms Ice Cream outlet, a Fanny Farmer candy store, and, off the main street, the Colony Home for wayward young women which furnished my mother with the weekly help of which she always complained.

I still get news of Syracuse from time to time from my younger brother Tony. Onondaga Lake, a site of the city's growth and its salt industry as well as a once popular bathing beach, has long been polluted and declared a "Superfund site," the only lake in the country with that dubious distinction. It is probably dead. A gigantic mall meant to be the biggest in the world—and ominously termed DestiNY USA—is in the works and terrible to think about. If my father were still alive I'd be hearing his refrain about progress. But even my two brothers, staunch supporters of Syracuse as our father was, have decamped to the suburbs. Past news was the shocking story that New York State's Canal Corporation, located in Syracuse, sold exclusive building rights along the state's entire 524-mile canal system (including the historic Erie Canal) to a Buffalo entrepreneur for the giveaway price of $30,000 with no other bids considered. That transaction is now rescinded by the assemblyman for my district. Somehow the canal project was linked to Syracuse's Inner Harbor marina project, the harbor being a former canal terminal south of Onondaga Lake and close to where DestiNY USA is to arise. The mall developer is the same person who bought the imposing building at Clinton Square that was Syracuse's federal post office, a happening that still astounds me.

The fine homes of James Street in its prime are today as vanished as the salt works and the central post office, as the summer family picnics of my childhood at Cazenovia Lake and Sunday drives. My father drove us to the rose gardens at Thornden Park near the university, to Liverpool for frozen custard passing the reconstructed French Fort overlooking Onondaga Lake, to Suburban Park near Manlius where the amusement park featured a miniature train ride through woods overlooking a stream so that I could fantasize future great journeys. Mostly we drove to Utica, to Gramma Cardamone's Queen Anne-style house, still intact and well preserved on Rutger Street, where she lived with her son Frank, his wife Lucy, and their nine children. Gramma was ancient and "old country," redolent of pungent smells, perhaps the very cardamom spice reflected in her name or, more likely, the collected aromas of all the years of her cooking for that large household over the big black wood-burning stove in the kitchen with the long oilcloth-covered table. In that house everything was special: pasta in bowls decorated with sailing ships that I imagined were Columbus's Santa Maria, Niña, and Pinta. And on holidays in the dining room with tables overflowing into the parlor, there were different flavored ice cream treats shaped like turkeys, pumpkins, fir trees, Santa Claus, bells, wreaths, angels. And later in the back parlor which adjoined the front parlor through sliding doors, cousin Teeney would play the piano as we all gathered and sang old-time songs like "Shine on Harvest Moon" and "Bill Bailey."

Just as strong as convivial memories is the piercing feeling of being lost in the world as experienced in the biting cold of winter twilight when my brother Jack and I trudged home to 2004 James Street after sledding on the hills at Sunnycrest Park. It brought back the homesickness I had felt when, too young, I was sent off to sleep-away camp. Just so, dragging our sleds homeward at dusk repeated the sensation of home being distant, perhaps unobtainable, a haven of comfort and warmth so far to reach.

I was the firstborn when my parents lived briefly at Prospect Street and I have the studio photograph taken of me when I could first sit up. I am in a white lawn gown adorned with a satin rosette below the neckline, and I'm wearing a delicate chain with a medal attached; I look solemnly ahead, one chubby hand in my lap, the other raised in surprise. I have a grave look, a far-off, wondering look. My dark hair lies straight around my round face and my clear, light eyes stare ahead under slightly raised brows. I am appraising whatever is going on. And that inward appraisal while looking out will stick for the rest of my days.

Memory, and so my history, doesn't begin, however, until I'm in the house at 2004 James Street that my father bought both as an advancement from his first house on Prospect Street and an investment. We, a family of five, had the first floor flat and upstairs was rented to tenants, a debonair family from New York City. The two-family is still there, a pleasant house with columns and flower boxes across the front porch. Upstairs, in my day, the six-windowed dormer was made fashionable with roll-up satin curtains in the Viennese style thus visibly marking the difference between our stylish tenants and us downstairs with ordinary window shades. The man upstairs was dapper, slim, always tanned and nattily dressed; his wife was a hearty, overweight, and chain-smoking woman who became a kind of mentor to my mother. They had one child, a very blonde coed with her own car who was a champion golfer and belonged to one of the best sororities at Syracuse University, the kind that pledged only one Catholic a year, if that. The family kept a German shepherd dog called Rex until the day he bit Jack in the leg and was banished.

Growing up I was unrealistically coaxed by my mother to emulate the paragon upstairs who was called Babe by her father after the incredible woman athlete of those times, Babe Didrickson Zaharias. Our Babe upstairs was always in the local papers for the tournaments she won. But I neither could nor wanted to be her. It was my brother Jack, instead, who would go on to become a golfing enthusiast and winner of amateur tournaments. The upstairs family was with us for years though I always thought of them as obviously meant for tonier settings and therefore temporary. My father, on the other hand, said they had made a smart move to come upstate—New York City, he used to say, was where people didn't live but simply existed, holed up in huge apartment blocks. He had other just as strong beliefs—in insurance policies, in White Owl cigars, in a whiskey drink called a hot sling to cure colds, and in the obliteration of unions and FDR as president. He simply and genuinely believed in progress and drove us to New York for the 1939 World's Fair where we saw General Motors' Futurama vision of cities to come—all highways, no neighborhoods, no people walking. That September Hitler invaded Poland; World War II began and progress would be to win the war.

Syracuse, my father said with pride, was the hub city of New York State, home of the annual State Fair, a baseball team, industries, and seat of a great university. Dreaming of California, he suffered through its winters, bolstered by his whiskey hot slings and long one-piece underwear but often suffering bouts of pneumonia. He'd compare his city to the disparagement of Utica, my mother's birthplace fifty miles east, and boasted of Syracuse's great companies: Crouse-Hinds, Carrier Corporation, L. C. Smith Typewriters, Syracuse China, Nettleton Shoes, Learbury's Mens Clothing. Carrier had endowed a new bubble-topped, 50,000-seat football stadium known at the Carrier Dome at the university. My father lived to be ninety-five but not long enough to hear that the Carrier Corporation was relocating in Asia, or to see the shabby, makeshift structure that is Syracuse's most recent attempt at a railroad station. He had always impatiently dismissed radio comedians who made gags about "the city where the trains ran through downtown." In his youth it had been the Erie Canal, where he had swum, that ran through town. A part of Syracuse since 1825, the canal was drained and filled in to become Erie Boulevard in 1925, the year of my birth.

Born in Syracuse, the eldest child of Sicilian immigrants, my father's pride in his birthplace was also connected to the city's recalling ancient Siracusa in Sicily whose name derived from the Greek word *syrako*, meaning swampy area, an apt designation for the new-world settlement as well. Both the ancient city and its new-world namesake, first named Salina for its briny springs, had grown from the salt industry born from those springs. A schoolmate at Lincoln School, who lived off James Street and used to roller-skate daringly down its steepest part, had an ancestor, John Wilkinson, who, in 1819, inspired by the ancient city, gave our city the name of Syracuse and became its first postmaster.

Syracuse was built on salt, says a history of the city, and the main downtown thoroughfare, Salina Street, still echoes that saline origin. The manufacture of salt was an important industry that would eventually die out, replaced by the Solvay Process Company producing soda ash from salt brine and limestone. When Alexis de Tocqueville came to Onondaga County in 1831 Syracuse was no longer "six scattered tenements surrounded by a desolate, poverty-stricken, woody country, enough to make an owl weep to fly over it" as described just a decade earlier by Col. William L. Stone. The difference was the advent of the Erie Canal, which, traversing Syracuse, had created commerce and a land boom. The Erie Canal spurred development and, as a leading backer of the canal, Govenor DeWitt Clinton was honored by Clinton Square, the city's main plaza. It was that erudite governor who gave many upstate settlements their resounding classical names: Rome, Utica, Pompey, Cicero. Camillus, Scipio, Manlius, Homer, Marcellus, Romulus, Ithaca, et al. I grew up hearing our city pronounced "Sarah-queues" (in the style of a David Harum, Syracuse's homegrown hero of the eponymous novel) and it wasn't until I learned Italian that I made it "Sear-a-coos" to sound like its model, the Siracusa of Sicily.

Life in my old neighborhood at 2004 James had its distinct flavor: when I was very young salespeople came to the house. I remember the well-rouged, jolly Belcano lady who sold my mother cosmetics and gave her facials with samples; the McCutcheon's man came from New York with a suitcase of beautiful imported linens; and the milkman drove up to the curb in front of our house in a horse-drawn wagon and delivered to the door milk in glass bottles with the cream on top. One of summer's great pleasures for us and our neighbors was sitting on front porches that looked out on the street and were furnished like outdoor living rooms complete with glider, flower boxes, and fiber rugs. Where I now live, the older houses still have ample porches, some still adorned with rockers, benches, or chairs tilted to face each other in a fake show of conviviality, as if longing to be occupied. But they never are—no one sits out reading or greeting passersby. As a fashion statement, one neighboring porch has not only stylish Adirondack chairs painted to match the house trim, but also a regular high-backed chair with the rush seat cut out in order to hold a flower arrangement. Porch life is as gone as hanging out wash on a clothesline to absorb the fresh smell of sunshine on bed linen. Porch-sitting is replaced by television viewers in airconditioned living rooms. And outside the sweet-smell of grass cut by hand-propelled lawn mower has been replaced by the clamor and evil odors of gas-driven machines that roil a summer twilight.

In earlier days a porch was called a piazza, an Italian word like Jefferson's Monticello where he, Italian-speaking, could sit, I like to imagine, and philosophize with his Tuscan friend Filippo Mazzei. On our porch, at 2004 James, I'd swing on the glider and read and wait for the neighborhood paperboy, the dark-haired McCormick boy who seemed to me the perfect version of radio's *Jack Armstrong, the All-American Boy*, and on whom I secretly had a crush. He'd come by on his bike and aim the evening paper right at the porch, never missing, and never giving a glance in my direction.

There wasn't much traffic in those days, but still my brothers and I were forbidden to cross James Street by ourselves. One day, with some pocket money my grandfather had given me, I did cross by myself only to find that Mr. Galloway refused to let me buy a Baby Ruth candy bar. Instead, he led me, mortified, back across the street to my mother who thanked him for refusing to let me buy anything if I showed up alone. So we were accompanied to Galloway's—mostly for an ice cream cone, but sometimes we sat at the marble counter on high, dark, bentwood chairs and had a soda or a hot fudge sundae. At home my mother made us her own concoctions called Black Cow (vanilla ice cream in root beer) or a White Cow (chocolate ice cream in ginger ale). Why "cows," we children would ask. "That's how it is," she'd say.

Fall and winter, neighborhood men like my father shoveled coal from cellar bins into their furnaces; there was a chute at the side of each house where the coal was delivered and shot down into the cellar. And then heavy ash cans were hauled out onto the curb. There was snow to be shoveled during the long winters, and I can still see my father beating at giant icicles—often waking us in the early morning to open our bedroom windows and jab fiercely at the icicles. He was a hard worker, rising early in the dark winter cold to go to work at the produce business he founded and that was always referred to as The Place. Three times he succumbed to pneumonia and I remember the doctor's calls at 2004 James and my mother crying. But he recovered each time, leaving us children with the conviction of his invincibility as well as his strong work ethic and sense of responsibility.

My mother liked fine things and it is strange to think of her in the dark, foreboding cellar where her domain had old-time cast-iron wash tubs, a washing machine with wringer, clotheslines, and an ironing board. It was there, on Mondays, that she did the wash, and then either hung everything outside on clotheslines, or inside according to the weather. Into the gloom of that cellar I was sometimes sent to fetch something from the back storeroom where crates from The Place colorfully proclaimed Ashtabula tomatoes, Sunkist oranges, Chiquita bananas, and shelves hosted all the back issues of my father's prized *National Geographic* magazines. The cellar was musty and scary and fed my imagination already filled with fairy tales about children lost in the woods.

A lot of our childhood play was on sidewalks where Jack and I rode our tricycles, and for a while we wore matching swimsuits to dash in and out of the front lawn sprinkler. Or we roller-skated, and sometimes had a lemonade stand in front of the house. But most of our play was in the back yard where I have just a vague memory of my mother's attempts at gardening—a marginal little border with flowers so skimpy and perfunctory that I don't recall them—marigolds, perhaps, or petunias, or snapdragons. They were simply incidental. It was the yard that registered with me for it was space for play, for invention. We played baseball, Redlight-Greenlight, tried to flood the asphalt area in front of the garage for ice-skating, collected fireflies in jars on summer evenings. And I played pioneer woman gathering the harvest of tall grasses from the steep banks at the back of our yard which separated us from neighboring houses around the block on Cook Ave. In the middle of our yard was a curious open-sided white-roofed structure (neither playhouse nor pergola) that my father was given by some customer and had placed in the yard, and there it remained, an oddity without seating or purpose, but where I stored my sheaves of harvested grass.

Between our house and the one next door there were steps on a bank almost buried in growth that must have at one time led somewhere; but in my childhood it was simply a mysterious ruin to explore. Even more compelling, once I passed through the hedge that separated our backyard from next door and crossed the yard, I got to the bushes with the snowberries that popped like small firecrackers when smashed by my foot. Behind the bushes, on another level, was the space between two garages that belonged to houses fronting on Hastings Place, a good hideout for our games.

I put on performances in the backyard that started simply enough with my best friend Kathleen and I dressing up and acting out movie scenes. But then I got ambitious and decided to stage the performances for the neighboring kids. My father sent up loading platforms from The Place for the stage, I pressed my brothers into acting service, Mom made lemonade and cookies, and I charged a penny a performance for spectaculars like wedding pageants or a replay of the 1936 coronation that had just taken place in England.

Sometimes I went to Kathleen's house. She lived around the corner on Hastings Place in a one-family house, and a favorite winter thing of ours was to jump from the roof of her garage into snow banks. Around the other corner on Cook Avenue was what we children called the back lot—a cavity of undeveloped land behind encircling homes where Jack played with the Quinn boys and had cookouts. And it was apparent even to my child's eye that Cook Ave was on a lower scale than Hastings Place or adjoining Melrose Avenue where another friend, Annette, also lived in a one-family house. I understood that a one-family house was a step up from a two-family. On the other hand, I was also aware that

15

my parents were a step ahead of our Syracuse relatives once they had left Prospect Avenue on the north side of town. My mother said, a different "element" lived on the north side and even then I recognized what a slur was.

That a prejudice against different "elements" existed was unexpectedly confirmed all these years later when a collection of correspondence from a deceased local politician was donated to the Hastings historical society when I happened to be there. He had been born in 1884 "of colonial stock on both sides" and was a graduate of Syracuse University with relatives and property still in Syracuse. A letter to him of 1912 from a Syracuse relative noted her fear that "Italians" were moving into the W. Colvin Street neighborhood and that would jeopardize the sale of his property there. The neighbors, she wrote, were quite alarmed at the arrival of the Italians. Now I knew that neighborhood in Syracuse to be one of solid middle-class homes as it still is to this day. Those feared as "Italians" were undoubtedly Americans with Italian surnames and with enough solidity and financial assets to be able to buy property on W. Colvin Street. Nevertheless, in the prejudice of that day they were "Italians" and so to be feared. Even more astounding to me was that today's political correctness prevailed over preservation of a historical record and the revealing letter was simply disposed of.

Everyone in those days seemed to have markers for people outside one's own group; Episcopalians, my mother noted, socialize and drink a lot; bargaining was jewing someone down; and the term Shanty Irish was frequently heard. I simply absorbed the class and neighborhood distinctions as well as the ethnic and religious ones. Still, nothing in the Catholic church I attended seemed as fine as the Lutheran Church covered-dish suppers my friend Annette on Melrose Avenue invited me to at her church so that, despite what the nuns told us, Protestants seemed a kind of elite to aspire to, as did my Irish friends with their easy-to-say names unlike my Italian surname, always mangled and mispronounced in school.

I was fair-skinned and light-eyed and hadn't the "olive skin" problem of which some Italian American women write. Yet I wasn't spared prejudice. Once Jack and I were playing in our backyard near the bank and someone from the Shuart house that fronted on Cook Ave but whose back porch overlooked our yard, called down to us: "Dirty Wops!" scaring us and causing Jack to break into tears. I grabbed him and ran inside where I told our mother what had happened. It was her finest moment. In the great act of our childhood, she threw aside her apron, straightened her hair and went out the door and up Cook Ave to the Shuart house to demand an apology. She got it. Old Mrs. Shuart said that her elderly, unmarried daughter was high-strung and unsettled by the noise of children playing, but it would never happen again. And it didn't. Instead, from time to time, I received pretty little handkerchiefs hand-embroidered by Mrs. Shuart with my monogram. Yet the call of "Wop" reverberated in me for a long time. For I had always wondered who I really was: American because I was born in Syracuse, or Italian because of our last name and the foreign grandparents with whom I couldn't speak? And whatever I was, would I always be called names?

Even as a child I could tell there was a difference between what I thought of as real Americans with their easy names and those of us who were American with "foreign" surnames. The intimations I had as a child of racial prejudice proved to have a well-founded base in American thought. Woodrow Wilson's *History of the American People*, written before he became president, contained a passage based on the census of 1890, the year my Sicilian and Calabrian grandparents immigrated to the United States: "Immigrants poured steadily in as before," he wrote, "but with an alteration of stock . . . now there came multitudes of men of the lowest class from the south of Italy and men of the meaner sort out of Hungary and Poland, men out of the ranks where there was neither skill nor energy nor any initiative of quick intelligence . . . as if the countries of the south of Europe were disburdening themselves of the more sordid and hapless elements of their population. . . ."

Lincoln School, which I entered in kindergarten and attended through ninth grade, drew from a mixed neighborhood: in the streets to one side of James Street we were from all backgrounds. But in the seventh grade Lincoln got the influx of grade school students from the streets on the other side of James and the difference was immediately apparent. Like a great dividing line, James Street had divided a Wasp neighborhood from the mixed one. I was intrigued with the new students and my ambition was to sit at their lunch table in the cafeteria and be accepted by girls with nicknames of Dodie, Bootsie, and Penny, and regular American last names.

Then a photographer from the *Post-Standard*, the morning daily paper, came to Lincoln School to take shots of students in various classes. I was selected for the science demonstration to hold a beaker and point to it at the lab table while Aldora Peck, Graham Shipton, and Jack South looked attentively at my demonstration. That photo appeared in the paper and was the highlight of my then life. I began to think that even with my name I was someone.

I was a reader and what books I didn't have at home, like my Nancy Drew mysteries, I got at the Eastwood branch of the public library. How I loved all those books containing so many wonderful stories! I'd lug home an armful of my favorite Richard Halliburton travel adventures where I learned of and longed for Petra the rose-red city half as old as time; or novels by Edna Ferber and I'd think, what could be better than to be a teller of stories! At home I had my *Child's History of the World* and *Child's Geography of the World* to feed my passion for knowing about different peoples and places. They provided me sufficient notion of an exalted

Italian history to make up for what I saw at the movies—the ludicrous, strutting Duce and his fascist bullies, or the American gangsters who always had Italian names.

Radio was a big part of our enjoyment. Every year a Utica relative, a prim little woman named Antoinette who wore eyeglasses, would come to listen to the Kentucky Derby on the radio in our living room. I could never imagine why and there is no one left now who can tell me. It was a regular occurrence, announced by "Tomorrow Antoinette will be here" and was just accepted as part of life. My own favorite radio program was *Let's Pretend,* a children's dramatized story hour introduced each Saturday morning to the strains of mysterious background music that I now recognize as Sibelius's "Valse Triste." I think I loved those radio stories as much—maybe even more—as the movies because I could imagine the characters and scenes beyond the radio set. The hardest penance I could think up for Lent was to give up listening to *Let's Pretend,* but in the years of my belief I did so. I also remember a mysterious picture that hung in my parents' bedroom of Christ's head with its crown of thorns as impressed on Veronica's veil when she had wiped his face while he bore his cross to Calvary. When one gazed at that somber painting, the eyes that had been shut, opened and fixed on you. Then they closed again. It was disturbing, mesmerizing.

My brothers and I attended Blessed Sacrament Church at the far end of Eastwood, a long walk to go to weekday Instructions. With Kathleen I sometimes played First Communion using Necco wafers as the Host. I always wanted the black, licorice-flavored wafer for its taste while she took the more suitable white peppermint wafer and I always wondered if what I did was a "sacrilege," a word and warning our Instruction nun was very fond of. Today I wonder if Kathleen and I actually shoplifted penny candy from the open cases at Woolworth's on our way to confession, saying that we could confess the sin and get rid of our guilt with our penance. Or did we just discuss the possibility? Her Uncle was a priest and she once told me that he said Italians were not as good Catholics as the Irish. I countered with the boast that my cousin Nicky was a nun but I continued to ponder the comparison since it really seemed to say that we weren't as good in all ways and it seemed strange for a priest to say that.

Or, on Saturday, my brother Jack and I would go to the Palace Movie Theater for a nickel matinee. If we had extra money we'd buy orange popsicles to see if we'd get the ones with "free" stamped on the stick, and sometimes we did. Once a classmate at Lincoln School named John d'Alessandro, a good-looking, happy boy, asked me to the movies; my mother said I could go but I had to take my two brothers with me, and so I did. I can't remember if John paid the nickel admission for each of us. Some sixty years later I saw him again at my mother's funeral when he came up to me and told me who he was—still smiling, nice looking, and causing me a quick nostalgic pang for our faraway childhood. And I recalled how in high school when a nice looking boy I had met skiing drove over to see me and parked his car briefly in the driveway at 2004 James. Briefly because my father stormed out and told him to leave. No other boy came to call after that.

When my first granddaughter was born and named Darla, I thought of the cute little girl with the Dutch bob and same name in the *Our Gang* movies I regularly saw as a child, as I thought every other American child did, too. It would be many years later, in my suburban married life, that I learned with amazement from an outspoken and independent-minded Wasp that she had not been permitted to attend movies until her teenage years. I thought her deprived. And then it was revealed by others of that background that the same was true for them. And more confirmed it! What did that mean? Was it a class thing that properly brought-up Wasp children were protected from Saturday afternoon movies? But what did they do instead?—have tea parties among themselves? It had never occurred to me (and somehow had slipped past my mother who was glad to have us out of sight for a while) that all children weren't going to the movies on Saturdays. Again I wondered, was it only the children with non-Anglo last names who went to movies? But I loved them!—Laurel & Hardy, Buster Keaton and Zasu Pitts, the *Andy Hardy* films with Mickey Rooney, Deanna Durban, Shirley Temple, the Ziegfeld Follies films with Dick Powell and Ruby Keeler, cowboy Tom Mix, even the *March of Time* newsreels. All except the occasional adult love-story films with Kay Francis or Ann Harding that I hated but sat through. For we went to the movies no matter what was playing, when not at the Palace it would be the Schiller Movie Theater near Aunt Grace's house when we played with our cousins. The Schiller was a smaller movie house, filled exclusively by children for a Saturday matinee. We were a boisterous audience and every so often the owner would shut off the film, come out on the stage, and tell us there'd be no movie unless we behaved. Then we did—who'd risk not seeing the picture?

Aunt Grace, my father's only sister, was married to Uncle Joe. He was a tall, lanky, dark-haired, good-natured and good-looking man who was born in Sicily, spoke a heavily accented English, and made wine in his cellar. I liked him for his good nature and beautifully kept backyard with its fruit trees, grape vines, and quadrant beds of flowers along pathways. He used to tell me about the days in the Prospect Street house, when he and Aunt Grace lived upstairs and my parents downstairs and I had just been born. I was to be brought up on what were considered modern feeding practices in the 1920s; authorities of that time warned against cloying motherly love, fearing it would not prepare children for the real world, which translated into the warning that infants should not routinely be picked up when they cried. Uncle

Joe would laugh when he told me of irritating my mother by picking me up when I cried, but I was glad that he was sometimes there to do so.

Occasionally, at night in our house at 2004 James Street I'd walk in my sleep. From the dark, dreamless continent of sleep I'd rise and wander through our first-floor flat as if in some strange unsettling territory, my disquietude violating the sense of deep quiet and repose that sleep signifies in tranquil lives. It seemed to confirm for my parents that, starting with sleep, I would be different in everything, that I could never be like glamorous Babe upstairs. In fact, my sleepwalking was prophetic. I was not only literally a "sleeper" in childhood when I walked at night, but even now as the term is used of any performance off to a slow, uncertain start and only slowly gaining acceptance. So my belated and surprising, unheralded and tenuous emergence as a writer marks me still a sleeper. It is my younger brother Tony who is the successful one—publishers come to him, he's never had the experience of a long-labored-over work being rejected. He is the master of his field, the authority on classic GarWood and Chris Craft wood speedboats; his books make money, are translated into foreign editions, and he is invited here and there to talk of them and sell out what he has along. I am glad for him for boats were always his love and now in his retirement from his career in education they have given him a new experience.

Though my childhood was a happy and protected one, my early sleepwalking and gnashing of teeth in my sleep seem to be signs that there were abysses of disturbance unseen by day that came out at night. No one perceived anything, thinking only that I was withdrawn and too given to having my nose in a book. It was a mix of shyness and intimidation: my father was a formidable authority figure who instilled apprehension. He didn't converse with us, he communicated best at work or with his golfing friends. At home he liked peace and quiet and that meant no talk at the table—meals were for eating not conversing while the food got cold. Once, in seventh grade, when I said my civics teacher wanted us to report on the news of the day that we discussed at the dinner table, he simply gave me his look and I kept quiet. We children knew our father's look. Pressed to report on something for class, I thought of all the years of the *National Geographic* magazines he had collected on shelves in the darkness of the cellar in lieu of his unrequited dream to travel. Africa, I reported to my class the next day, we talk about Africa.

Though both my parents had the typical second generation urge to Americanize as fast as possible and leave the traits of their immigrant parents behind, they still bore the impress of those parents in subtle ways. Children, they told us often enough, owed their parents respect. Duty, not love, was the operative value in their expression toward us. My father had an admirable sense of responsibility and carried it out both in his family of origin and with us, his new family. He wasn't, however, good on explanations. He knew what he had to do, had it all in his head, and saw no reason to explain his orders to us. "Here, sign this," he'd say pushing some official paper toward my brothers or me. It would be railroad investments in our name or insurance policies or bonds bought on our behalf, but he never explained. He looked after us in his own way, but there was no exchange. Now, so late, I realize that in my own way I have taken after him by showing affection not verbally but in dutifulness. I keep things in order, look after my three daughters with reminders and messages for their own good, get my work done on time. But I am not, as he was, the Boss. I brought up my own daughters to be independent minded, not to sign papers blindly but to read and question everything. And now as the oldest, the scholar, would say, I am hoist by my own petard.

Just as my father never imparted financial information, so my mother never divulged her recipes, housekeeping advice, or the facts of life. Mom, who liked emulating her acquaintances and giving me advantages like summer camp, dancing and music lessons, horseback riding, and dreaded Shirley Temple permanents, was deficient where it counted most: instilling in us children that we were loved and valued for ourselves rather than for keeping up with other children. What my mother neglected totally were the personal, intimate expressions of mothering: expressions of love, interest in my reading or creative play, preparing me for womanhood. In adopting American ways and the modernity of the twenties, both my parents lost the old-world family cohesiveness and unity of their parents. They had discovered a whole world outside family—family was no longer the fortress one stayed immured in; there were other attractions like business and social success, a country club and a Corinthian Club, material possessions.

"Smile!" my mother was always admonishing me on how to be popular; "Hold in your stomach!" So I grew up both dutiful and rebellious. When, in my senior year at Syracuse University I was elected to Phi Beta Kappa and told I could have one person accompany me to the celebratory dinner, I felt it should be my father who had, in his own way, taught me to work for what I wanted.

Yet, in subtle ways, I stayed a sleepwalker. Part of the sleepwalking effect was not being street-smart—unaware even that there was a Black community in Syracuse, not being sharp but dreamy and unfocused—and always, it seemed, waiting for my friend Kathleen who, no matter what we agreed, was always late while I never figured out until now that I needn't have waited.

At some point in my life when I heard of The WASP Cookbook, it made me think back to Lincoln High School where, while boys took shop and learned to build and repair, we girls learned to sew and cook in home-economics class. I remember learning to make Welsh rarebit, tuna fish casserole, prune whip, tomato aspic, chipped beef on toast—all things we'd never eat at home, but which I told my mother about. It turned out that she herself, once, had attempted to go Wasp in her early days of marriage by serving my father creamed chicken on waffles. Once and never more; he had certain rules: Sunday was for spaghetti with meatballs (the word *pasta* was not used and no other form of it ever appeared) and he could get testy about the tomato sauce if it was too bitter, too thin, too thick, too cooked; a chunk of iceberg lettuce to munch on was all he wanted—no mixed salad; white fish or kidney beans were served in a broth of oil and garlic; strawberries were never to be crushed as a topping for ice cream and fruit in general was not to be promiscuously mingled in a "fruit cocktail;" and only Italian bread was ever to be placed on his table. American bread, which Pop disparaged as cotton batting, was reserved for our school sandwiches. "Take out the soft part," he'd command us children about Italian bread, "eat the crust, the soft part's no good." I didn't know until I learned Italian that the word for the soft inside was *mollica*—our very surname. And his witticism, repeated each year when he brought home melons from The Place was "I can't elope with you . . . oh, honey do."

Mostly my father was a silent man at home; he wanted peace and quiet around him. His work life was challenge and bustle enough. He relaxed by playing golf in the summer and he bowled in the winter. He had wintered the storms of his poor, early life and made it through to the house on James Street, and his children would be college educated although he had never finished high school.

I admired both my parents—they were handsome and well spoken. He, the boss of his own business, was successful and able to provide well for his family, a self-made man who had advanced himself in life by his own efforts. She, a great socializer and appreciator of the finer things in life, had a handsomely bound complete set of Dickens stamped inside with her maiden name, the pages still uncut, that occupied a living room bookshelf. In the dining room an open cupboard displayed her collection of English bone china teacups and Italian figurines. My mother knew fashion and our home was modest but in good taste because she read the right magazines and had learned from an older Utica relative who was her mentor. She dressed well, set a good table, knew brands and how to shop for bargains in quality things. She had brass altar candlesticks, picked up at a secondhand store, wired for lamps. At house sales she could always ferret out a treasure of one kind or another. From the Flora B. Smith mansion came our handsome solid bronze fireplace set and from the sale at Judge Hiscock's place, along with gold-leaf framed mirrors, she got the little Italian phrase book that would eventually play such a part in my life. My mother learned as she went by copying her "betters." Artful were the two windows flanking the living room fireplace where she had installed glass shelves for her collection of African violets. When she heard from me that my friend Annette's mother took her to ballet lessons and had bought her a diary, she did the same for me, adding occasional outings to Schrafft's that, with its cool, dark, refined interior and chicken-pot-pie lunch, was a superior treat. And then, in our teenage, she taught Kathleen and me to play bridge, a superior skill to have later at college.

The bus stopped across the street from 2004 James and as a young girl I was able to go by myself to the YWCA to swim on Saturdays. And later, with transfers, I could get to any part of the city for my piano lessons, for high school sorority meetings at various homes, or even to Drumlins way beyond the university for ice-skating and skiing on those gentle, rounded slopes formed by glaciers in the ice age. I liked going downtown and meeting Kathleen for a movie, or listening to Tommy Dorsey records at the record store, buying Karmelkorn, and charging a purchase to my mother's account at one of the department stores and giving the clerk my address on James Street.

It was in our small living room at 2004 that I sat and wrote at the secretary desk, looking up in concentration so that my gaze always fell on a nearby wall plaque, a reproduction of Sebastiano Ricci's *Adoration of the Magi*. There I would compose, write, invent "The Convent Chimes," a monthly newsletter of which I was editor when I was a high school student at the Convent School. I still recall how irritated at her superior airs and how mortified at my ignorance I was when an upper schoolmate, interviewed by me for my column on reading, gave Izaak Walton's *The Compleat Angler* as her favorite book and I had never heard of it. She was of the family that founded in Syracuse the original Schrafft's candy line and restaurant chain. She and her sister were driven to school by a chauffeur in a limousine and I can still see them as I sit on the front steps, taking off the roller skates by which I had gotten to school, and pulling up my hated stockings to fasten to my even more hated garter belt. They wore a more fashionable version of the graceless uniforms the rest of us wore for they were allowed to have a dressmaker create theirs.

Was it the diary, presented to me with the injunction "It's to write in," that made me a writer? I lived much in my imagination as a child and writing was its continuation. I made up backyard plays, I wrote poetry and especially remember one dedicated to the magnificent big tree that stood at the top of the steep bank that separated our yard from the Shuart property. When I was twelve I wrote a piece about a dress in a store window for a contest the *Herald-Journal* was sponsoring and won the dress. I seemed to have become a writer on my own in a tentative manner without a mentor and before writing conferences and workshops or the academic support of an MFA program in creative writing came into being. I know that my mother never intended that the diary she bought me to keep up with other girls would be my entry into the world of writing. But it wasn't only the diary; there were my library books and the *Let's Pretend* broadcast on the radio every Saturday morning that fired my imagination, and even the backyard performances. Growing up and living was my material.

But I know now that though I got good grades in school and was put ahead a class and won a four-year Regents scholarship for college, growing up I seemed to know nothing of importance, not about political parties except that Syracuse always voted Republican, nor about the depression and WPA, poverty and segregation in America, or why it was that in America some Americans were more American than others. I read a lot, memorized, and did well in school. But I didn't know how to speak to my immigrant grandparents because I didn't know Italian or even wonder why I didn't. I didn't know about close confidences with my parents, I didn't know how to be happily away from the family house in order to be happy at camp or college. I was in my own bubble of limited experience. Soon enough I had begun to distrust organized, authoritative religion to which as a twelve-year-old, without conviction and the necessary fervor, I was routinely committed through the act of Confirmation. Though my brothers are true believers, my parents were reticent about religious faith: my mother saw weekly church attendance and occasional communions as a kind of insurance policy to be kept up just in case; my father had the long-ingrained anticlericalism of Italian males and railed against the crooks in the Vatican and all their kind. I tried once to express my doubts to the priest hearing my confession. I needed counsel, understanding, deep thoughts. Instead the priest snapped back angrily, "You are not to doubt, you are to believe!" And so I do: I believe with Keats that it is our present life that is our "vale of soul-making;" there is no other.

What else I knew from early on was the imaginative fantasy of stories from my beloved six-volume *Bookhouse*. Then, the exhilaration of skiing, the beauty of Latin, the music of Mozart, and the ambivalence of wanting to leave home while yearning for it. I seem to have been born homesick. It is a feeling deep within, recurrent, abiding and, I think now, what's behind all those homes of mine set up and then left. For I seem never to have reached home safe. I felt I was nothing in the scheme of things and yet that perhaps I could be something in a new scheme. I knew what was expected of me, knew I couldn't comply. I felt alone. I knew that at some critical moment the very self of me did not fit either my family or the place I grew up in, that I would always be rebuffed or have to find my own place in the world, yet that I wanted love, that I would do anything—cross the Alps!—to get it.

It was at the end of my high school years, when my father's produce business prospered, that he sold the two-family house at 2004 James Street and bought a newly built house at 1305 James Street, moving us up in the world. Across the street from us, prominent on a slope that occupied almost a whole block, was the then imposing Georgian mansion of the Catholic bishop that had first been the residence of a Mr. Cogswell, president of the Solvay Process Company and, at his death, acquired by the Catholics of Syracuse for their bishop. Now, no longer the bishop's residence, like an insider's real estate joke, the site has filled up with bland structures known as the Bishop's Condominiums as if His Excellency were in fact the developer. But our house at 1305 remains as it was.

It's a romantic Tudor-style house with stone facing and casement windows, peaked roofline, and an archway leading to the back. In our day a man came to take care of the front lawn and do the plantings my mother ordered—a long row of tulips bordering the driveway in the spring followed by geraniums and begonias summer to fall. For the new house the old upright piano which was in my bedroom at 2004 was replaced by a baby grand in the living room. And on the wall above it hung a portrait of my father, self-made man, wearing in his lapel his Rotary Club pin, a badge of honor signifying his achievement onward and upward. After experiencing the constraints of a single bathroom at 2004, where someone seemed always to bang urgently on the door when I was taking a bath, it was luxury to move to the new house where there were three bathrooms plus a third-floor maid's bedroom and bath, which Jack immediately claimed for himself, having changed in adolescence from a skinny weakling into a tall and handsome athlete.

Home reading came through the mail: *Saturday Evening Post, Ladies' Home Journal, Life,* and continuously until his removal to a nursing home the *National Geographic* magazine, my father's favorite. When I married, among his gifts to me was a subscription to the *Geographic* and over the years it followed my many moves, to Italy and back. Now I live in a drastically changed world—all the romance of Richard Halliburton's adventures and the lure of diversity have vanished, the strange worlds and people that used to fascinate from the pages of the *Geographic* have been overlaid with American influence in the world. As early as 1946 Erich Auerbach in his *Mimesis* had said, "There are no longer even exotic peoples." What would he say now?

There, at the new house, I began to subscribe to *The New Yorker* and to listen to Texaco's Saturday broadcasts from the Metropolitan Opera House in New York. And I chanced upon a Sunday morning radio broadcast called *Invitation to Learning,* in which a group of intelligent and witty people discussed great books. It was wonderful—there was finally conversation in the home and I was the listener. In my new room I no longer hung the picture of a cheerful, buoyant, dark-haired young girl striding across a country field holding three different colored balloons in her hand and looking out from the frame with a smile. She had been with me at 2004 but I no longer wanted her company. I was a different person—I wore girdles and pancake make-up. I liked being in the new house and equated it with my mother's finer things in life and where our Americanization was achieved. And very soon I was away at college.

My real time had been at 2004, and my real time in Syracuse was coming to an end. My childhood family's long-ago move to

1305 James Street was my father's final exercise in upper mobility after having become a member of the Rotary Club and joining the Syracuse Country Club at Lake Oneida. I looked forward to this instant gentrification but there were losses, too, for me: no more walks to Eastwood, no more neighborhood or backyard play, no more blissful summer days reading on the front porch. Instead there was a sunroom for my mother's plants and a La-Z-Boy recliner in Naughahyde for my father. It was the first move in which I was involved, packing up my books and things, but it would be far from my last; there have been more than a dozen since.

My father was perplexed by my wanting to leave Syracuse and study in Europe. He was even more so when I married an Italian, but he came to love Antonio Barolini and with him spoke the Italian that he had never given his children. My parents remained at their James Street home until very old age when, first my father, then my mother went into a nursing home. I saw him last when he was ninety-five. Though his mind often wandered, he knew me and said I looked good, relaxed; he complimented me on my Loden coat. Then he lost his train of thought, believed he was at his golf club, and fretted about his foursome not being called to tee off.

All the years I lived on James Street, and even as a literature major at Syracuse University, I had never heard from any professor of my street's connection with Henry James. It is only now that I know that James Street was named for Henry's grandfather, William James, who emigrated from Ireland at age eighteen in 1789 to settle in the United States. In Albany, New York he lived out the traditional American success story by becoming one of the wealthiest men in the new nation and patriarch of a notable family. William of Albany (to distinguish him from his well-known namesake and grandson, Henry's brother William James of Cambridge, Mass.) had as one of his many enterprises an interest in salt manufacturing in the area that would become Syracuse. From salt, the elder William James moved on to become a land speculator, indeed to have been the major purchaser of the whole settlement in 1824 for $30,000. Together with his partners, the Messrs. Burnet, Hawley, McBride, and Townsend, they owned great portions of what became the heart of Syracuse. City streets are named for each of the developers but James Street was by far the grandest. It was from the income on such real estate speculation that Henry James's father and ten siblings were able to live comfortably all their lives and still be able to make bequests to their own descendants. In his autobiography Henry reports that he once visited Syracuse and asked the agent in charge of the properties from which his father had derived his comfortable lifelong income when his father had last visited. He's never visited, the agent answered. That was a different case from that of his own father, William of Albany, about whom F. O. Matthiessen in his book *The James Family* has this quote: "When old Billy James came to Syracuse," a citizen recalled, "things went as he wished." Henry James, in Syracuse to inspect the family property, was the visitor who wrote home that he had been driven "along James Street, the 5th Avenue of Syracuse," one of the handsomest American streets he had ever seen, and "named after our poor Grandfather." By then a successful author, he turned over much of his share of his inheritance to his sister Alice and still continued to live handsomely from his writings.

I think now and then of Henry James, his connection with my street, birthplace, and the nearby suburb of Jamesville named for his grandfather. I think of the changes in that handsome street named after his grandfather. And I think of Henry's expatriate life and conflicted loyalty as he wrote from Europe to his friend Charles Eliot Norton in Cambridge, Massachusetts: "It's a complex fate, being an American. . . ." And it seems to me now that those fine New England gentlemen didn't know the half of it—the Italian half of being American.

My Mother's Wedding Day

It seemed a remarkable coincidence when the mail brought me a page from a long-defunct Utica newspaper called *Il Pensiero Italiano*, which gave an account of my mother's wedding day, for it arrived just three days before the anniversary of that event. The paper was dated November 17, 1923; it was sent by a researcher of Utica's Italian American community whom I had met the past summer at a book reception and who seemed interested in my mother's Utica background.

The Italian Cultural Center where the reception was held had been a convent for the nuns who taught at nearby St. Mary of Mt. Carmel School and adjoined the Italian church of the same name on Catherine Street. It was the heart of where my mother had grown up. She had been schooled by the nuns and married from the church, so it was a homecoming of sorts for her to be at the reception with me.

I had used the old Italian church and its school as part of the background for my novel, *Umbertina*, and, at the time of writing, had researched several Italian language papers published in Utica in the first part of this century. Somehow I had missed the account of my mother's wedding day. I had found the death notice of my grandmother (on whom the character Umbertina is based) in *La Luce* and remember reflecting ironically on how she, who had been the brains and energy and determination behind her family's success in founding the business that gave them their well-being, was remembered in death only as the wife of her husband Angelo.

Angelo, in an earlier obituary, was credited "through his honest and untiring work" with launching his sons into business "and opening for them the way to that excellent place in everyone's esteem that the family enjoys today. . . ." The newspaper account ended with a cordial salute: "to Signora Nicoletta, his good companion, and especially to his sons Frank, Sam, and Joe, who have so worthily followed the paternal example, we offer our most sincere condolences."

What an irony, I had thought as I read the account in *La Luce*—another woman subsumed under her husband's name while her own achievements are forgotten and her credit is that of a faithful spouse who gave her husband seven children. Another bit of women's history sacrificed to prevailing patriarchal attitudes. For all my childhood I had heard the legend of how my formidable grandmother had willed her husband to this country from the old one, had initiated the business which she ruled over through her sons, and had bossed her daughters into becoming the women they were and whom she married off with her only instruction to them that they never come back to her with tales about their husbands. Loyalty, first and foremost, she told them. A matriarch, she educated them for patriarchal ways.

Perhaps strong women always think they are the exception and make sure that their daughters aren't set up for failure by having dangerous notions of their own strength or worth; or perhaps strong women who become domineering mothers want to keep their uniqueness to themselves and don't educate their daughters to be competitors. Or perhaps the daughters themselves let their roles fall to them through inertia and default; they're born, after all, when the struggle had already been accomplished; they're the privileged whose wedding days get written up as my mother's was.

That newspaper account arrived just in time for me to send it to her on her anniversary (and I say her anniversary because only she, now, is aware of it; for several years my father has been gently balmy and immobile, fastened into a wheelchair at a nursing home where he imagines he's about to tee off for a golf game, and knows nothing of anniversaries or his children and grandchildren, though he does recognize his spouse and chuckles when he sees her, saying to his fellow inmates lined up with him against the wall in their wheelchairs, "This is my wife.") The date, however, also marks my own wedding anniversary.

No one remembers that; I became widowed years ago and I am no longer thought of as having a wedding anniversary. But I haven't forgotten it and every year when my mother's anniversary comes round, I too remember being married. Perhaps that is why the arrival of that wedding announcement from the Italian paper was so portentous to me: it reminded me of a former life, a family life with a husband and home and children in it, and how I had deliberately linked my wedding day to my mother's and even chosen to have the number of children she did. It is absurd that I, so temperamentally different from my mother, should have duplicated her external life's milestones. Or is it?

I read Italian and she doesn't because I made it my business to go back to the country her parents came from and reclaim it for me. So I called my mother in Syracuse to read her the Italian paper's story. "It's called 'The Happy Nuptials,'" I said, "and is about you, the cultivated and most gracious Signorina Angela, who was united in marriage to Signor Antonio, one of the most important businessmen of Syracuse."

My mother laughed self-consciously and I could picture her smiling happily. "How flowery!" she said; "I never heard of such a paper."

"The wedding," I read, "was celebrated in the Italian Church of St. Mary of Mt. Carmel in Utica and the bride, a gentle flower of beauty and goodness, is one of the most esteemed young women in the higher rank of Utica's Italian community."

"Send me the copy and I'll have someone up here write out the translation for me," she said.

"I will," I promised, without going on to read her the entire piece. Embedded in it was something that later gave me pause: "the bride was accompanied to the altar by her mother, Signora Nicoletta, widow of the late Signor Angelo. . . ." I attached a note to the newspaper account asking my mother why she had never mentioned being given away by her mother, and mailed it off to her.

"All I could think of as I was reading about the wedding," I told my eldest daughter Linda by telephone that evening, "was that my poor mother was going from one powerhouse—her mother—to another, her husband."

"But that's monstrous!" came the strong reaction. "Her mother led her to the altar?"

"Well, her father had already died, you see."

"But she had three older brothers! It's grotesque to think of her being given away by her mother!"

My own reaction had not been to the unseemliness of my grandmother giving my mother in marriage but that the transfer of power from parent to bridegroom had actually occurred with the true holder of power—in this case, the mother, who was in fact the dominant force in the family even before the father's death. I imagined the old woman telling her three grown sons, "I'll take care of this myself—I'll take her to the altar." And they, as always, obedient, respectful, dutiful. An Old World touch to my mother's New World wedding, I imagined.

But why was my daughter reacting so strongly? Why did she call it monstrous? Hadn't I been to Jewish weddings where both father and mother escorted the bride down the aisle? I thought it a nice touch; why should the father alone accompany his daughter to the brink of separation? All the better, thought I, that a deserving woman like my grandmother had got a chance to show equal authority. In fact, I imagined that perhaps in Calabria, where Angelo and Nicoletta had been born and from where they emigrated to the States—there, in the Magna Graecia of antiquity where female deities reigned and women like Nossis of Locri were acclaimed poets, women had some visible power and that it might well have been the custom for a mother to join a father in giving a bride away, and then doing it on her own if the father were deceased.

Just before the event I am relating I had been in Italy and had gone to visit the Museum of Magna Graecia located in the city of Reggio Calabria to see, among other things, the famous bronzes of Riaci, the two huge ancient sculpted warriors from ca. 500 B.C., which had just been fished out of the Ionian sea and put in the museum in all their grandeur.

But what most moved me at the museum was the visual link from antiquity with the matriarchal figure who had been my grandmother: display cases in room after room disclosed an abundance of female divinities and female votive offerings; terra-cotta statuettes of the female figure celebrated in charming, natural poses, or venerated as the creative life principle. Remarkable were the tablets from the excavation at Locri representing with poetic delicacy scenes in the story of Demeter and her daughter Persephone.

What did it mean that this joyous evidence of female importance in the life of Magna Graecia led inexorably to a final chamber where the two magnificent Riaci bronzes, huge deified warrior statues, stand in all their male power and supremacy proclaiming (if there were any doubt) who really ruled the world and engaged in the battles of dominance? The male figures are almost identical and in stances which suggest that each once held a now-missing shield and lance. They are statements of might, of perfect masculine strength. They are beautiful. They are larger than life, while the female divinities are smaller; the bronze warriors are unique, the female representations are of an astounding proliferation, and were to be seen everywhere from Sicily to Naples as part of daily life.

Given my exposure to that abounding female presence in Calabria from the earliest times, I was willing to speculate that in the Calabrian colony of Utica, New York in the twenties it would not have been outlandish for a mother to have outranked her sons.

But what was discomfiting was the conjectured image of an old-fashionedly garbed and ungirdled matron in black, with strands of loose gray hair escaping from a top-knot on her head, going down the aisle at the side of a thoroughly modern, Americanized and horribly embarrassed daughter (who was going to Paris on her honeymoon!). No wonder my mother had never told me this part of her wedding story. She must have suffered the indignity in a kind of swoon of disassociation from the scene and then suppressed the memory ever after. No wonder I had never seen a newspaper account of my mother's marriage.

But I had seen the bridal picture: they are a handsome couple. She is attired in a fashionable flapper-style gown without, however, any trace in her of '20s spunk; her eyes are demurely downcast over a huge bouquet, her hair is not yet bobbed but long and marcelled into tiers of waves. Her eyes are brown and his are, too, but hers are the brown of docile, romantic dreaminess, while his are more restless though his features are young and naive looking. He hasn't yet the look that goes with his later cigars. But at age twenty-seven, a self-made man from Syracuse, he has the satisfaction of being able to give his Utica bride a honeymoon abroad. They will sail on the liner *Aquitania*, she with an elegant wardrobe and a red leather diary from Brentano's stamped in gold MY TRIP, and he with a month's supply of cigars.

I have my mother's travel diary. Her first entry: "Beginning of the Big Trip or Honeymoon Expedition as called by my husband. We stayed at the Commodore Hotel in New York, the last word in Luxury and Beauty, as majestic as a royal palace." (They stayed there five days and nights waiting for the *Aquitania* to arrive and saw Broadway shows, St. Patrick's Cathedral, well-dressed crowds, and the Columbia-Cornell football game.)

But the crux of the travel journal is another matter. Skipping over her delight with New York restaurants and the next few days of transatlantic seasickness to get to what happened when she arrived in the land of her parents, I find the pages blank. The journal does not go past the sighting of Cherbourg.

Yet the honeymoon trip can be filled in from snapshots in the family album. There, in the wilds of Calabria, is the bride cowering in the corner of the carriage which took them to her mother's village. She looks stunned, dazed. One can imagine the shock after the Commodore and *Aquitania*. How did she get there in the first place? I can't imagine her suggesting they call in at her mother's village after seeing Paris and Rome. It was probably my father's sense of duty. But one look was enough for him, too. They stayed overnight and then fled. My grandmother never could understand how anyone as flossy and inexpert as her American daughter would have wanted to go there in the first place.

But as for my mother's wedding day, even if she had wanted her eldest brother Frank to give her away, what say would she have had against her strong-willed mother? How many stories had I heard from my mother of her mother the boss! My mother, modern and cultivated and gracious as she may have been, didn't stand a chance when it came to her mother and so I was prepared to believe that willy-nilly, the gentle flower Signorina Angela had indeed been accompanied to the altar by the ample, monumental figure of Signora Nicoletta.

For hadn't the story, many times told me by my mother, gone on to relate how at her wedding dinner ("a sumptuous reception," said the paper, "in the home of Signora Nicoletta") my mother had been faced with her first trial: seated beside her at the head table my father had looked down at the plate of lasagna served him and said, "I can't eat this." Did she wonder in that instant if all her married life was set out before her? Fortunately, she is not a reflective person. She aims to please. In her gown and veil, she got up from the wedding table and went to her mother's kitchen where she ordered a dish of spaghetti for the new boss. She has always understood about power and standing in with those who have it. She had understood in her mother's house, and now, about to go to her husband's in Syracuse, she got the message again.

It was also because of that wedding-dinner story which I've heard through the years glossed with commentary ("See! Haven't I always catered to him, right from the start!"), that I was willing to believe that my mother had made one last concession to her mother and gone up the aisle with her before she transferred her allegiance to her husband. It would have been perfectly in character. It would also have been in character never to have mentioned the indignity, despite the many recitals of the wedding dinner. She would have endured the last show of her mother's power, but she would never have talked about it; it was too close to the bone. Also, as I was coming to understand, it was not merely a question of defiling Emily Post's notion of decorum, but an issue of matriarchs, patriarchs, and self-determination with which she had never grappled.

On the other hand, being the perfect wife to her husband, starting from the moment they sat down to the wedding dinner, was something she could tell over and over again. I sometimes wonder if she realized that any chance she might have had of declaring herself released from her mother's authority was squelched in the bud by her immediate complicity with the new authority on the one day when she might have prevailed. It was her one chance not to cater. She didn't take it.

In her account, my mother always points out how accommodating she was, and how demanding Pop. But that seemed normal, even noble, in a man's world. And in 1923 what other kind of world could she imagine? It was her mother's power that she resented and that seemed improper. Ready to serve the man who would support her, she was part of American normality. She could chafe under a matriarchy, but willingly embrace as right and regular the codes of patriarchy. She was part of her times although, unremarked by her, her times also included suffragist women who got the vote and the first manifestation for an equal rights movement. Unknown to her, feminist Alice Paul was of her times and every bit the American my mother thought she was in her up-to-date clothes.

My mother's actions of the twenties don't surprise me; it's my daughter's reaction in the present day which does.

"That's really revolting," she kept repeating with deliberate emphasis. "Poor *nonna!*" she said in commiseration.

I began to wonder not about my mother but my daughter. Why, in fact, was she so revolted at the mere thought of a mother giving a daughter in marriage? It was the archaic presumption of "giving" over someone from one's possession into the possession of another that bothered me, not which of the parents performed it. But that was not what my daughter was objecting to. Self-determination was never the question (for in our age, the marriage partners can give themselves to each other, if they wish, and write their own vows), but only the fact that convention—Anglo-American convention, at that—was not observed.

It was my daughter's horror at what she saw as a breech in the order of things that got my attention. She willingly suspended

judgment on the old patriarchal tradition by which a man transferred, in a social contract called marriage, an item of chattel to
another man in consideration for the other man taking over the
expenses entailed in maintaining and supporting that chattel. She
didn't question the implications of the ritual itself, it seemed, as
long as the proper roles were kept. What bothered her was the
switching. She was troubled at the woman doing what in her
thinking was reserved to the man. She herself, alone of my daughters, had a traditional wedding and it was my father who gave
her away in the absence of my deceased husbamd. She wore my
wedding gown and her grandmother's veil. She liked to think she
was doing things correctly, observing tradition. But what tradition? Whose idea of correctness?

When I visited my mother in Syracuse a few weeks later, I
wanted to hear from her what had actually taken place on her
wedding day.

"Oh, no," she said, "my mother didn't give me away—it was
Uncle Frank! That Utica newspaper is wrong. In fact, I could tell
from the writing—so ornate, so Italian!—that they got it wrong.
When I got back from my honeymoon the only clipping I saw was
one from the *Syracuse Journal* about my wedding cake."

So much for my theorizing about the place of woman in a culture of Southern Italy going back to the Magna Graecia of antiquity! Unless, of course, the writer of the piece for Utica's *Il
Pensiero Italiano* was not actually present at the ceremony but had
reported it as it might have taken place. Perhaps there actually
was precedent from the old country for the bride to be escorted to
the altar and given away by her mother. I wanted to know.

"So Italian!" my mother had declared deprecatingly of the
wording of the *Pensiero* story. Her words echoed her long-abiding
repugnance for anything that was backward, as she termed old-
country ways. She told a story that illustrated what she didn't ap-
prove of in "those people." It was about someone on the Syracuse

side of the family who was ugly and uncouth and known as The Wop because she kept rabbits and pigeons in her backyard. When the time came to cook them up for special occasions, she herself did the slaughtering and dressing. She was the kind, my mother said, who kept a goat during Lent in order to have it for Easter dinner: even the head was split and stuffed and nibbled on; nothing was wasted. My mother always made a show of shuddering in the telling.

It wasn't until I lived in Rome and had the delicious Roman dish of roasted young spring kid that I knew it was no more barbarous to eat goat than lamb or ham. It was all in one's associations; my mother's associations with "Italians" had been as something to get past on the way to being acceptable Americans. As my mother recounted the story of The Wop it became a cautionary tale and the moral was that if we didn't push away Italian ways, we, too, would be "those people." In fact, the story concluded, even the woman's little granddaughter was that way—when she once found a hurt bird while playing, instead of tending it as an American child would, she had taken it to her grandmother and asked her to cook it for her.

I could understand my mother's terrible fear of being linked with such peculiar stuff. And how the very words of the *Il Pensiero Italiano* about her wedding day seemed threatening.

A friend of my mother's had written out the translation for her, noting that an expression used to describe the bridal party encircling the couple—*facendole corona i fratelli Frank, Sam, e Joe*—did not "fit in" and so she left it untranslated. On the contrary, *facendole corona* (literally, making a crown around them, but meaning, simply "to encircle") is a perfectly standard Italian expression. What didn't "fit in" for my mother and her friend were even the word patterns of a culture different from the dominant Anglo-American one they were used to and which seemed the only "right" one to them.

My mother's initial pleasure in my revelation of the old newspaper account of her wedding day had dissipated. She began to disassociate herself from it as she had, all her life, tried to keep herself at a distance from her Italian background. It was "Italianness" that she resented, rather than her being co-opted into an anglicized conformity that led her to question the background she came from. The pressures were great—she and my father wanted only to blend into the American way when they married, and so they did.

I find it sad that what must have been the highlight of my father's life was his being accepted as a member at a golf club which had a restricted membership and normally did not include "Italians," any more than Jews, Blacks, or Asians; that he made the grade and was accepted for what he actually was, American, must be behind his still teeing off for a golf game as he sits strapped in his nursing home wheelchair. It is his most sustaining memory. Not his birth in Syracuse, New York, but country club golf made him an American. Behind his anger and my mother's perplexity at my wanting to explore my Italian heritage—something that never interested my brothers—was the fear that I was jeopardizing all they had built up. "You've always been different," my mother chided me.

Was it that perversity that made me not relinquish the newspaper story of my mother's wedding day?

I was curious. "Where is the *Journal* story about your wedding cake?"

"Oh, that disappeared years ago! It told about my wedding cake which was made by Josie Penizotto's father here in Syracuse. The *Journal* sent a photographer down to take a picture of Josie standing beside the cake and the headline said, "Worth Her Weight in Cake" because the cake weighed as much as she did—and you remember her, she was always big even as a girl."

"I'd love to see that picture. What date was it? I can go to the library and find it on microfilm."

"Oh, I don't know—I wasn't in Syracuse when it came out. Aunt Grace gave it to me when I got back from my honeymoon. Why is that so important to you?"

"It's interesting—I remember all my childhood hearing about that cake. How love birds flew out of it when you cut it. I'd love to see a picture of it; it's part of our family history."

She was skeptical. "What difference can it make! Now you're going off to the library to look through some old papers! I thought you came up here to see me!"

"Come with me to the library—it will be fun for you, too."

But she wanted none of it. And when I came back from my fruitless research, having looked through the files of the *Syracuse Journal* for the days preceding the wedding date in November 1923, she said, "Maybe it wasn't the *Journal*, after all. Maybe it was the *Herald* or the *Post-Standard*."

Wouldn't she have remembered where and when that piece appeared? After all, it was a most unusual cake and quite an item to appear in the paper. The cake had been ordered from Penizotto's bakery on the Italian north side and not only was it huge, but the cake itself rested on a base of solid nougat. Embedded within the cake was a special cage that opened when the cake was cut into at a trigger point to release two turtledoves. That fabulous cake had been present in my fantasy since childhood. I used to think the birds were real and I would wonder about their dirtying inside the cake, or smothering. I finally asked my mother about them: "Silly!" she laughed at me. "Those birds were mechanical and were made to fly out when I released the spring by cutting the cake at just the right spot."

What a romantic story. Who wouldn't want to see a picture of such a cake? It made me think of the old Penizotto bakery with its smell of almond-paste and anise, so different from a vanilla-flavored American bakery. Life is complex: some Italian things, like Penizotto's bakery, were obviously all right to my mother.

"Why do you put so much importance in a cake?" she asked me irritably. "You're not going to write about me, are you?"

"No. I'll write about Josie."

I should never have said that. My mother likes to be the center of attention even when she denies it. I began to suspect that she knew more about the right paper and date than she let on. After I returned from the library a second time, having found nothing again, she told me, "Maybe it wasn't the week of my wedding that it came out, maybe it was the Sunday after. I remember it was in the rotogravure section."

I gave up another trip downtown to the library. For whatever reason, my mother wants to keep her wedding cake to herself.

On another wedding day I was back in Syracuse at my mother's house. The youngest daughter of my younger brother was being married. Though her surname is Italian, she is (through her Irish mother) blonde, blue-eyed and the personification of the perfect "Americanness" my mother aspired to. The only "Italianness" that seeped into my niece's life was at my mother's bountiful table where she found some dishes like cannelloni or stuffed mushrooms. Long ago my mother had learned, in her words, "to tone down" her repertoire of solid Italian food like calamari sauce with pasta, the real ricotta pie with wheat which heralds spring, or even roast lamb rather than ham for Easter, in deference to the American women her sons married and to the American grandchildren they gave her. Very early, indeed on her wedding day, she had learned to cater.

But at her granddaughter's wedding, my mother saw what it meant in the long run to downplay her heritage and identity—to swallow herself and give in to the others. It was an Irish wedding, as she said; none of our relatives living in the same town and bearing the bride's same maiden name, were invited. When I asked my brother about this, he said, "We never see them." And I answered, "But at this stage of our lives, weddings are the place to see them." He shrugged and walked off; like his mother he doesn't like to make a fuss.

Was it an Irish touch, or unconscious irony, I whispered to my daughter, that at the exit from the church each of us was handed a balloon on a string so that, at a signal, they could all be released into the air looking like nothing less than so many sperm wriggling up into the sky to prenote an awesome fertility for the unaware (I think) bridal couple and for the certainly unaware no-nonsense mother of the bride.

At the wedding reception the Irish jig was danced and the place swarmed with the Irish takeover—hard drinking and boisterous jokes. It didn't look like any of our family affairs.

The next day at the breakfast table, going over the wedding with those of us who were staying with her, my ninety-year-old mother said sadly, "It's as if my whole part of the family didn't exist. That wedding was all Irish!"

I had what my husband used to call (in Italian) a rush of tenderness for my mother. I considered how hard her position had been in the generation just after the immigrant parents. She and my father had the most difficult balancing acts; they had to separate from the foreign into homegrown. She tried, and she did it with style despite the losses. "Maybe you can remind your grandchildren who they are on your side—tell them family stories," I said to her, "as well as make them your mother's Christmas cookies every year."

"I guess you're right," she replied with an air of regret. "My sons' wives don't even have olive oil in their homes! None of their children know anything of their Italian side. Only Johnny is interested in me and will sit with me and ask questions."

"Oh, Linda is like that, too," I said, "Linda is interested in family history. . . ."

"You don't have to explain me to everyone," Linda, who had been testy and imperious over the weekend, broke in. "I do historical research in my career, and further back than just this family! I don't have to have my position defined by you."

I considered. My eldest daughter, in her own way, is a powerhouse. I have always been struck at the circumstance that, in a sense, created her a virtual Athena: though Linda was born in the United States and has a normal birth certificate here, when she was only two and a half, we returned to Italy and registered her, as was required, in the Municipality of Rome where we resided. Years later when a birth certificate was required for her passport as she returned to the States for college, it was found that through a clerk's oversight she was entered in the Rome registry as the daughter of a father, but with no mother. Nothing, today, surprises me less.

Daughters can be unrelenting of their mothers. And then at a certain age, certainly by my mother's age, they begin to forgive.

After all the years of a life spent trying to downplay her Italian roots, my mother was regretting that she hadn't passed on her own mother's heritage to her sons' children. She would have had to have made that resolution long ago and to come to terms with the image of that old-fashioned, unstylish Italian mother dressed in black whom she was determined not to be. She would have had to accept the immigrant mother, embarrassing as she was to the modern woman my mother wanted to be; she would have had to have the self-determination to forge her identity and hang on to it long ago, hopefully by the time of her wedding day. Now she is no longer that young woman, she is old, older than her mother ever got to be; now she has regrets for what was lost.

Again I asked my daughter about her own strong reaction to the now disproved story of my mother going down the aisle with her mother.

"It would have been horrendous at nonna's American-style wedding to have had that old black toad ruin everything!"

"Is that all?"

"NO! All I could think of was you—how I once felt so in your power that I was suffocating, that I would never be able to relate to a marriage partner because of you."

And I understood. All of us daughters have to unmarry our mothers.

Zio *Filippo at Summer Camp*

Imagine this: it's a heavy, humid summer day even in New York's Adirondack Mountains. My brother Jack and I are at adjoining summer camps at Eagle Bay on Fourth Lake. Cedar Cove is for boys and Sunny Ledge for girls. These are very tony camps and are more indicators of my father's business success than my wish to be there. The campers and counselors dress in uniform every day but, since the day I am now recollecting is family visiting day, we are wearing our special dress outfits.

I am a pudgy preadolescent in puffy brown bloomer-shorts (old-fashioned even then in the late 1930s), a yellow camp shirt with a brown neckerchief tied under the collar, a brown beret, yellow socks, and brown shoes. My brother wears the grey-green colors of Cedar Cove and I envy him, hating my tacky colors.

On this day we will perform all our sports activities before the guests. My parents are coming with someone special: *zio* Filippo, my father's uncle from Rome, is in the United States on a visit made possible by the small bonus he received on retirement from his long-held clerical job in the Italian Naval Ministry. He's come over to visit his brothers and sisters. They all, save him, had left Sicily and come to the United States in the 1890s. *Zio* Filippo, instead, emigrated to Rome. There, like many southern Italians, he worked in the government's swelling bureaucracy. He would have had to swear allegiance to the Fascist regime when Mussolini came to power in order to hold on to his government job; but now he is safely retired with a pension, meager as it is. The year is 1937; in a few years Italy will be an ally of Nazi Germany and at war with the United States.

I had never heard much about Italy as I was growing up in Syracuse. My grandfather, *zio* Filippo's brother, was not someone I could talk to. I neither understand his broken English nor the Italian he spoke to my father. And for reasons that I knew nothing about, he came to our house only once a year, on Christmas day, my father's birthday. Escorted by my Uncle Benny, Granpa always brought my father a box of cigars. Then he'd sit in the sunroom with his overcoat still on, have a shot of whiskey, say to my brothers and me, "You-ah good-ah keeds?" He'd give us each a nickel and then leave. I understood without being told that my father did not welcome him. The difference between Granpa and my father was all too visible. My father had started his own business, belonged to Rotary and a country club—was, in short, a regular American.

Granpa was a foreigner; he looked poor with his baggy trousers, his stumbling gait and general run-down air. He did odd jobs at my father's wholesale produce business at the regional market. But what he had done in life, who he was, how he had come to this country, what he had worked at, and what he thought was all a mystery to me.

When I met grandpa's brother, *zio* Filippo, the mystery only deepened. *Zio* arrived in Syracuse accompanied by my father, who had scheduled some business in New York with his food broker in order to be at the dock to meet his uncle when he arrived on the *Conte di Savoia*, one of those regally named, grand Italian ocean liners of another day.

I was impressed and surprised at the sight of *zio* Filippo as he got to our house on a late winter day. He was a dignified older man, well-dressed in a grey suit topped by an overcoat with velvet lapels and wearing a snappy fedora creased in the crown and with upturned brim. A Borsalino, I would later hear my father commenting on the hat in an impressed tone to my mother. He was very different from my grandfather. *Zio* Fillipo had grey hair and a thick grey moustache; he stood erect, looked somber and regal like the king of Italy who sometimes appeared in the *March of Time* newsreel that preceded the Saturday matinees my brothers and I attended at the Palace Movie Theater eight blocks away. Of course, *zio* Filippo was taller than the little king, but the way he carried himself was much the same. Years later in high school Latin class I would learn it was called *gravitas romana*. I was confused: how could someone from Italy look so impressive when I had always heard that Italy was poor and backward, that the United States was superior in all ways?

It couldn't have struck me then, but certainly does now, that there was a difference between the Italians of Italy and the Italians in America. Despite their advantages, Italian Americans seemed to have lost the grace and dignity and *saper vivere* that Italians naturally have. More than an ocean seemed to separate my grandfather from his brother, beginning with their name. *Zio* Filippo spelled and pronounced his surname one way, my father and the rest of us were stuck with the way the name, slightly misspelled, had been registered when my grandfather went through U.S. immigration—a small difference, perhaps, but still something that symbolically separated us.

I did not see *zio* Filippo again until he turned up at my summer camp. He had been in the States for months. Where did he stay? I wonder now. With my grandfather? But where did Granpa live? I never knew; we had never visited him. At some point *zio* went off to visit his sister and two other brothers who, along with other family members, had settled in Philadelphia. I had no idea who that family was, had never seen them or heard their names. My grandfather, long a widower, had always been in Syracuse as was true of his four sons and one daughter. My father was the eldest and, in fact, the family head since it was he who had started the business that employed the others.

That he had displaced his own father was the point of a story he sometimes told us children of why we lived in Syracuse, with its terrible winters and heavy, humid summers instead of in golden California. At age nineteen when he started his own wholesale produce business, he had come in contact with growers and shippers all over the country, but mainly California, and he formed a dream of that state from which the fruits of the earth came to him in railroad cars. He decided that that was where he wanted to live.

He had been his mother's favored child, the one who worked as a paperboy, shoe shiner, errand boy, and writer of letters for the illiterate *paisani* who wanted to send money back to the Old Country. Most of his earnings he gave to his mother and she in turn gave him a chop or steak while the others ate beans and escarole. She was sickly, however, and died in her forties of heart disease. As my father told the story (and it became solidified into family lore), on her deathbed she called him, rather than her husband, to her side and charged him with taking care of the family. My father kept his promise to her and gave up his dream of California.

Eventually, I learned something more: after his wife's death my grandfather lived with another woman for the rest of his life and this displeased my father, who refused to meet her. Still my father showed *zio* Filippo a great deal of respect and attention.

But I have deviated from the occasion when *zio* Filippo showed up at summer camp. He is caught in home movies that my father took that day. I see him, erect and impassive of mien, as he stands on the field watching us campers at archery, his gaze following the women counselors and gravely taking in their bloomer costumes and exposure of leg. One counselor, in particular, has caught his attention—she is also the swimming instructor and when we move on to our diving exhibits, she is there in her bathing suit, again under *zio* Filippo's serious scrutiny. Was he scandalized by the grown women in shorts and bathing suits, or did he admire their ease with themselves?

The movie camera then finds us all at Jack's camp where he is in the riding ring and is given a ribbon for performance. Jack is a good athlete despite being a very slight, scrawny, dark-complexioned boy who looks more like a Naples urchin than an All-American camper. Thinking back all these years I wonder if *zio* Filippo was comparing the camp sports program to the *ballila* Fascist Youth rallies where obstacle races were run and manly prowess showed off. Was he recollecting black-shirted *fascisti* and their performances hurtling through flaming hoops on motorcycles, or gathering under Il Duce's balcony in Piazza Venezia to roar their approval of the conquest of Ethiopia? Or was he wondering why my grandfather hadn't been invited on that visit to the Adirondacks camps? Was he thinking, what kind of man disowns his father? What does family mean in this New World? Have Americans a new way of living, free of family ties? Could he imagine that camp was a place families paid to have their kids off their hands for the summer? What did he think of Americans seemingly guileless in the world while Europe armed for war? Or did he find us truly blessed in the New World, free of ideologies and free from having to stiff-arm salute a dictator as was happening in his country?

I'll never know since I couldn't speak Italian then and even if I could have, it is unlikely I would have conversed on such subjects with either *zio* Filippo or my father. After he returned to Rome, and when the war did come we lost word of *zio* Filippo. But when I saw Vittorio di Sica's powerful postwar film *Umberto D*, I thought of our relative in Rome. The film's opening scene is of aged pensioners in Rome demonstrating and crying out for an increase in their miserable pensions even as they are dispersed by the police. The film focuses on the aged Umberto D who had worked forty-five years at the Ministry of Public Affairs and was trying to survive in the harsh conditions of postwar inflation that had reduced his pension to almost nothing. I thought of *zio* Filippo as Umberto D. Had he been reduced to such hardship?

Eventually we learned through Uncle Benny, who had heard from the Philadelphia relatives, that *zio* had died sometime after the end of the war from pneumonia. He had marched hatless in a religious procession on a windy day and caught a chill that eventually killed him. Hatless? I wondered. Had he had to sell his elegant Borsolino?

I myself finally got to Italy to study and there I met my future husband. With him I learned Italian and Italian ways. One I taught my children and now my grandchildren here in the States where I again live: when dandelions turn from golden blossoms into fluffy, silvery seeds, you hold the stalk close to your lips and blow a long, drawn-out "*Fi -lip- po!*" aimed at the fluffy seed head. That final hard syllable blows the winged seeds in all directions. I do this with each new grandchild and each time I think of *zio* Filippo, his long-ago visit, and the questions born from that visit that, like dandelion seeds, got dispersed in the air and blown away.

The Spinsters of Taos

One summer in Venice I finally met the person, a friend and countryman of my husband's, to whom we were to have sent a postcard from Taos, New Mexico, seven summers earlier. Antonio spotted his friend and introduced him to me in a splendid courtyard on the island of San Giorgio just across the lagoon from the Ducal Palace on the occasion of the Campiello Literary Prize awards, and over drinks and an elegant buffet I explained why he had never gotten that card from Taos.

When Antonio was American correspondent for Turin's daily paper *La Stampa* and we were living outside New York, he had been chosen, along with nine or ten correspondents from other countries, as recipient of a State Department grant to travel in whatever part of the United States he wanted to know better. Antonio chose to see the West—and I went along for the ride. And, silently and secretly, along the Big Sur coast, among the Sequoias and in Monterey, on Fisherman's Wharf and at the rim of the Grand Canyon, and all the other places where we were met and taken in hand by volunteer hosts sponsored by the travel grant, I held in reserve my own particular project—a visit to Taos, just the two of us in a rental Hertz on all the back roads of New Mexico.

What lured me to Taos was its association with D. H. Lawrence, for there, some forty years earlier, Lawrence and his wife Frieda had lived in a ranch outside town and it was to Kiowa ranch (out of all the places in the world where they had lived) that Frieda had taken his ashes after Lawrence's death in the south of France.

How could we get as close as the Grand Canyon and not push on another four hundred miles to Taos to stand in the wild hills Lawrence had loved and visit the mementos of his stay there? The chance would probably never present itself again since the child I was expecting would make any such future jaunts unlikely, and then Antonio's post could (as subsequently happened) be changed.

Antonio himself, for motives not purely literary, liked the idea of dropping in at Taos, too. Aside from seeing the American Southwest, he relished the thought of sending a postcard from Lawrence country to that friend of his in Vicenza who had become a distinguished Lawrence scholar and had written the definitive Italian biography on the writer. This friend has spent years scanning and seeking and sorting evidence on everything pertaining to Lawrence and his group. He had devoted his scholarly life to Lawrence, constructing a marvelous monument to him. He had seen the England where Lawrence grew up and had visited all the haunts of the Lawrence's various sojourns in Italy, Sardinia, Sicily, and France. But to Taos, to the place where, say the Indians, beats the heart of the world and where Lawrence met the New World and rests forever, he'd never been.

The Lawrence scholar's life was that of Vicenza: simple, orderly, and provincial, the complete antithesis of Lawrence. It was, indeed, the very paradox of his affinity for Lawrence that intrigued Antonio and led to the whole idea of the teasing postcard.

Except that we never sent a postcard for we never got to the ranch. I think it was the undercurrent of maliciousness in Antonio's idea that boomeranged onto us and did the mischief. But *he* has it that we were bewitched on the way—put under a spell by the concentrated, possessive jealousy and fury of old erotic obsessions in those women he calls (whether they were or not) the spinsters of Taos. They are the women who hovered about Lawrence in his lifetime and then tried to make his memory their own special and exclusive province.

We should have been forewarned of exotic doings upon reaching Santa Fe; it was clear that we were no longer in the standard USA with its practical bent; it was more like the Mediterranean world where the warm dramatic color of Catholicism is peopled by devils and miracles and is rich with superstitions and lore. What was the sanctuary of Chimayo, where we stopped on the way to Taos, but the Old World with its suffering saints and amiable sorcerers and, marvelous to say, even a pit of miraculous mud in a dirt-floor chapel off the main altar? We could have been in Sicily.

The light and color of the wide New Mexican sky and those great spaces of blooming sagebrush were exhilarating as we continued our drive through the Sangre de Cristo mountains. I regaled Antonio with bits of the reading I had been doing on the Lawrences in Taos—how the formidable Mable Dodge Luhan had willed them there in the first place; how Dorothy Brett, daughter of Viscount Esher, had left England and followed her idol Lawrence to New Mexico as a kind of worshiper and *bonne a tout faire*, where she not only annoyed Frieda by her ubiquitousness, but later wrote a book entitled provocatively *Lawrence and Brett*. The master and his handmaidens—the women detesting each other and vying with one another to trim Lawrence's red beard or bake his bread. If Frieda had been jealous of Mabel, whom she called a "culture-carrier," and Mabel had been bothered by Brett and her ear trumpet (always there, she said, like the eyes and ears of the Lord), both Mabel and Brett loathed Frieda for she was, after all, Lawrence's wife. The ladies have all composed memoirs contradicting each other but all written, as Aldous Huxley observed, as though they had invented and patented the one and only Lawrence.

We passed the time with such literary gossip; when we reached Taos it was well past one and we went straight to the town's starred restaurant, a charming Spanish colonial place captained by a cordial giant in a chef's cap, who briefed us on its history and prepared us a fine lunch. We were in Taos; we could feel a difference in the air—lighter, purer, exhilarating—and we looked around us knowing (having been more than prepared to know) that everything was meaningful. My attention was taken by a group of elderly women at an adjoining table conversing with animation about women's rights—this in a time before the women's movement had been born. Then in a flash of intuitive certainty, I recognized them. They were, surely, part of Lawrence's circle in Taos, they were the adoring women who had contested among themselves for his attention and had driven Frieda to fury. They who had been the devotees were still here in Taos, the tenders of his ghost. One woman above all dominated the group; this she did by the high-U authority of her English accent, by her carrying voice, by the very ampleness of her person, and because, finally, she used a microphonic gadget (hung on a cord about her neck like a lorgnette) in front of the mouth of the person addressing her to transmit, by wire and battery impulse, the sound of what was being spoken into the hearing aid fitted into her right ear.

I nudged Antonio. "It must be Brett, she was deaf," I whispered, feeling like an archeologist who's come across some relic in his digging, a potshard, a tool, and feels hot on the trail of greater glory.

We studied the English lady over luncheon. She was pontifical and pacific in the self-sufficiency of what seemed a perfect egoism. Her face was bland and childlike, her hair white and her motions slow—not slowed by age but by the tranquility of whatever serene philosophy glowed behind her small eyes. A nose that might once have been sharp and prominent was softened by the vastness of surrounding flesh and the plump mountains of her cheeks. She was sacerdotal in her calm and dignity and the green Indian tunic she wore, laden with heavy silver Indian jewelry; the matching band around her white hair conferred, I imagined, rank on her—chief of the surviving Laurentians. She was, as only an

English gentlewoman can be, extremely well-suited to her Indian garb. She dressed with natural éclat in the Indian manner just as, in other eras, certain aristocrats loved to wear laurel bands and togas. Her solemnity and grandeur were augmented, if anything, by her hearing aid. With the mien of royalty she moved her microphone from one mouth to another, following exactly what conversation she pleased, eliminating what she disliked from her existence. I watched with pleasure and no little envy as she switched from one busy mouth to another then silenced them all, so to speak, by putting the microphone into her tunic pocket and returning to what must have been the supreme satisfaction of her majestic separateness. The waitress had come with the lunch check; while the others clucked and chattered among themselves and scurried in their bags for bills and coins, the Englishwoman sat impassive and still, having nothing to do with the business at hand. Like a flagship escorted by busy little tugs, she was then convoyed out, the genial chef himself bowing her to the door.

As we were finishing, Antonio asked our waitress, an intense woman with the nervous vitality and quickness of lean, pared-down middle age, if she could give him directions to Lawrence's ranch just outside Taos. She started, seeming as ill at ease and evasive as if he had asked directions to her home. "It's very difficult to get there," she told him. "Maybe they can give you directions in the bookshop next door."

We went to the bookshop and there we saw our Anglo-Indian lady seated in an overstuffed armchair and completely filling the tiny premises, like a combination of Queen Victoria and Sitting Bull. She looked around imperiously with her placid gray eyes and stared impassively at us. I should have liked to speak to her, but I was, I'm afraid, intimidated. And then my attention was taken by Antonio, who was asking the bookstore woman what route would take us to the Lawrence ranch. The woman's voice took on a shrill note as she visibly lengthened her neck and aimed her answer at him, "Oh I wouldn't advise you to drive there!" she said with conviction. As she spoke, another woman clerk, pale, thin, with large black eyes, looked our way and joined in, "The road is terrible—it's quite impossible." And then everyone seemed to be talking at once, we pleading that we had come to Taos just to visit the Lawrence place no matter how bad the road leading there, and the bookstore ladies just as vigorously trying to discourage us. Only the woman in the armchair sat inviolable and impenetrable in her silence; perhaps she divined our errand, perhaps not; she gave no sign.

In the midst of this a customer entered the shop, an acquaintance, evidently of the bookstore woman who said to her, "These people want to drive out to Kiowa! I've been trying to tell them what a bad road they'd have to take and how isolated the ranch is."

"Why don't you visit the Kit Carson house," the newcomer said to us. "He lived here, too, you know, and his house is just across the street."

We were irritated at this inverse zeal. At this point it began to dawn upon Antonio that this was a conspiracy of all the aging females in Taos who wanted Lawrence only for themselves. It was they, he speculated, who at town meetings voted against repairing the road to the Kiowa ranch; they who swore the citizens to secrecy about directions; they who started the diversion of a Kit Carson museum.

With my Italian husband muttering, "Who was Kit Carson?" we did in fact go across the street to the Carson house to plan our next move. If Kit Carson was no part of Antonio's Veneto childhood, he was instead definitely part of my American one. I forgot for the moment about Lawrence and plunged into the Western memorabilia of the museum while Antonio waited in the antechamber where the usual souvenirs and reading matter were displayed. The person sitting behind these wares, as he later told me, was smoking and at first he couldn't get a clear glimpse of her. Then she emerged from behind her smoke, and from the thin, wrinkled arms that hung from her sleeveless dress and the puckering of skin about her elbows, he would have put her at an advanced age, but her face was so colorful, her hair so blonde, the ribbon through her curls so gay and youthful, the jangle of bracelets and necklaces so insistent that he realized with a pang that he, European, was no longer a judge of women. As he remained transfixed by his doubts, she, splendid in her self-assurance and self-preservation, asked if he didn't want to visit the museum.

He replied glumly that actually he wanted to visit the D. H. Lawrence ranch and asked without much hope if she could direct him there. As foreseen, she waved his request away like an indelicacy. "Actually, as far as Taos is concerned, Kit Carson was far more important in its history than D. H. Lawrence. It was Mrs. Luhan who got him to come here, you know, but he never really did fit into the life around here. Oh, the tiffs she and Frieda Lawrence used to get into! Everyone who knew them has written a book about his stay here. I've got copies of most of them right here and maybe you'll find something you want. I think you'll find it much more satisfying to read about him than to go all that way to the ranch. There's really not much to see—his typewriter, an old hat, that sort of thing, you know."

By the time I came out Antonio had a plan. We'd go to the Chamber of Commerce and put it on the line: we wanted to get to Lawrence's ranch. Actually, we didn't have to insist at all, for in the office we found a young girl of seventeen or eighteen who may never have read Lawrence but who whipped out a map and penciled the route to his ranch with the greatest dispatch. As we drove out of Taos, congratulating ourselves on our endurance, a large black cat sauntered across the road from the left to right side.

Antonio looked at me, began to speak, and then stopped. "You're not superstitious, are you?" I laughed. He shook his head and stepped on the gas. The highway was smooth and empty, the sun high, the country endless. We passed an adobe village where Indian women were washing in a stream and baking in outdoor ovens while the menfolk sat in clusters, taking the sun, chatting. Sicily again.

"Wretches," Antonio said as we sped down the highway toward the line of wooded mountains. "There's no better countercharm to the spells of those spinster-witches than to curse them in turn. Miserable witches! Terrible road, indeed!"

After about fifteen miles we came to the turnoff and started up a dirt road where, after a mile or so, we found an inconspicuous sign with, in small lettering: To Kiowa Ranch, D. H. Lawrence Shrine; a larger sign read Property of New Mexico University. The dirt road had now become little more than a path, rocky and rutty and bounded on both sides by woods, with nothing to be seen ahead but more woods. The car bounced and rocked on the miserable road but we continued slowly and carefully. "We're almost there," Antonio said. "As soon as we've looked around, we'll send off a card about it to my friend in Vicenza who thinks he knows everything about Lawrence."

But all I could think of was, how did they do it in those days? How did Lawrence and the women get up and down such a road in the winter to go to Taos for food or mail? And I thought of them up there at the ranch with their eternal woodchopping and scrubbing and mending. But while I mused as to how the Lawrences had survived, Antonio was getting visibly more and more apprehensive. The car was all but unmanageable, there was no sign of human life anywhere, and we were miles from nowhere, and me in my "condition." Gathering us in were the fathomless depths of surrounding woods and it was as if we were alone in the middle of the great continent in utter solitude. Above, the sun still shone reliably, the sky was brilliant blue and empty of clouds. There was, now and then, the call of a bird or chirp of an insect but mostly there were signs all about us and in the air of the great summer thirst. There was thirst in the trees, in the dusty road, on the rocks, at the road edge on the weeds and flowers.

"Won't this road ever end!" Antonio was muttering when we came to an old wooden house in a clearing and got out to investigate. It wasn't Lawrence's ranch, it was a university field station and completely empty. It was then that we discovered our rear tire and its inner tube in shreds—we had been driving on the rim, for how long we had no idea.

I looked at the sun; it was still fairly high, but eventually it would set. "Let's just turn around and go back the way we came," I told Antonio. "If we drove up with the tire like that, we can surely get down again."

"And what about Lawrence!"

"It would be silly to go on ahead, the other tires might go, and then we'd really be stuck. It's easier to go down than to continue up—we don't even know how far."

And so, maneuvering slowly, we got to the highway where help came and our tire was changed. But without a spare or a jack in the trunk and with night coming on, we didn't dare attempt the road to the ranch again.

The sun was just fading behind the wooded hills when we returned within sight of Taos. And there at the fork where the highway meets the main street of town, the big black cat reappeared and crossed in front of us again, this time from right to left.

"The spell is lifted now," Antonio said with a bitter laugh. "The witches have won! They wouldn't let us approach Lawrence's ashes, those spinsters of Taos. Now they've got him again, all to themselves."

I sometimes remonstrated against what I consider that Venetian streak of bizarre imagination indulged in by Antonio to explain ordinary happenings. But this time all I said was, "Maybe you're right."

We had to get back to Santa Fe at once, pick up our luggage, and proceed on to Albuquerque to leave by plane for home. The car, as we drove away from Taos, seemed liberated; it hummed happily along the road back through the Rio Grande canyon, and the night sky was luminous with stars. I thought of the English lady sleeping serenely under patterned Indian blankets, her microphone and hearing aid on the night table next to her bed. I thought of the other elderly maidens of Taos, all sleeping, all tranquil now that, at least for the moment, no other curious trespasser would assault the silence guarding the ashes of the mentor of their dreams of love. And Antonio thought of his friend across the ocean in Vicenza, undisturbed by any pangs of envy that we, and not he, had succeeded in getting to Lawrence's ranch outside of Taos.

When I gave this account of our Taos trip to Antonio's friend that night in Venice, he listened attentively, his brow furrowing with anxiety as I described our approach to Kiowa Ranch. It was a tense moment for him in the game of literary one-upmanship. As I concluded, he breathed out a deep "Ah!" smiled and nodded his head saying, "So you didn't actually get to the ranch?"

"No," I said. "But when you do, send a card."

II Abroad

A Fish Tale

It was a long time ago, just a few years after the end of World War II, and there I was, a bride in mist-wrapped, sodden-aired, graying and bombed-out Vicenza in the north of Italy. With my husband Antonio, Vicenza-born of a Venetian paternal line, I was temporarily ensconced in a walk-up, top-floor apartment carved from an old palazzo where Antonio's family had lived and only one sister now remained. The apartment was a modest one with a front room, a kitchen, and bedrooms off a long corridor that led to the bathroom, but it harbored the remains of a better, more prosperous time when there had been a family country place with handsome furnishings.

We were married in early November; there was a sense of chill humidity everywhere; dresser drawers stuck with the dampness, closets smelled moldy, the antiquated bathroom with its long pull chain and unlit water heater was disheartening. And as winter approached, the Palladian charm of the town so prettily traversed by its three rivers and fringed by the Berico hills was canceled out by the daily difficulties in the aftermath of war.

There was that damp chill everywhere despite the valiant little woodburning stoves. In the center, the palaces that lined the main street seemed desolate and cold. The Bar Garibaldi, which was said to have once been the seat of the literati, was occupied by pool players. When we went to see a film, it was in an old abandoned church where we sat in the choir in our coats, shivering in the drafts and watching our breath form in front of us.

The year before, I had arrived in Vicenza for the first time to spend the Christmas holidays with Antonio's family. I was alone in Italy, a student in Rome, and not yet very familiar with the language. Despite the austerity there was a sense of exhilaration about the future and of people ingeniously making do. Railroad cars were still in short supply and I was lucky even to get on the train to Vicenza where I stood the whole way. At that time I knew Antonio very slightly (having met him when I first got to Italy through a letter of introduction from a fellow journalist), but it was worth the long trip north from Rome not to be alone at Christmas.

Antonio worked as a journalist but was known as a poet. In his hometown he had a reputation not only as a literary figure, but also as being distantly related to one of the town's noblest families. That combination afforded us, shortly after our marriage, an invitation to dine with a leading industrial family named Z——, whose fortunes had greatly increased in the war. Perhaps the invitation was also curiosity on the Z——s' part concerning the young American wife of an established bachelor-about-town. That would have been something to talk about and see firsthand in those days in Vicenza.

Antonio, being a poet, had no notion of advising me about the formalities of such an invitation and I did not know the customs. I was new in Vicenza, spoke little Italian, and was very raw. I had already had comments from Count Giustino Valmarana, a friend of Antonio's, when we met up with him one day while walking.

"You need new shoes," he said, indicating my footwear. I had on what were called "pixie boots," soft red leather with a V-cut in back, American, and, I felt, very much smarter than the dowdy, stout shoes the *vicentini* were wearing.

"They're not broken," I said, lifting my foot to point to the V-cut in my pixie boot, "that's the fashion."

"Americans!" he snorted.

And I found it odd and unsettling to be deferred to by elderly maiden ladies. I had been brought up at home in Syracuse to let my elders pass through doorways before me. In Vicenza, after Antonio introduced me to a white-haired older woman who carried an old-fashioned patent leather handbag on a chain that reminded me of my grandmother, I was flustered when she stood back and insisted I pass in front of her as we entered a cafe. But why? I asked Antonio later. "Well," he said easily, "you are the signora, she a signorina—she was deferring to your married state." Or, I considered, showing how important it was for a woman to be associated with a male no matter what her own accomplishments or her seniority might have earned her on her own behalf.

The evening of the Z— dinner, I got out a favorite dress from the trousseau my mother and I had shopped for together. I had two designer outfits, both by Claire McCardell, one a navy suit with collar, jacket placket, and pockets outlined in white double stitching like that on denim jeans (unknown then in Italy); the other a full-skirted wool dress in an expansive full-blown orange color. The dress had deep pockets, a neckerchief type collar that tied, a belted waistline, and full monastic sleeves for thrusting one's criss-crossed hands in as nuns do or for pushing up to expose an armful of bracelets.

Those two pieces were the most expensive clothing I had ever had, and my mother, shopping with me at Flah's, then the fashionable store in Syracuse, had been wary. But I had prevailed, carried away by the sheer chic of the name—Claire McCardell designs were new and innovative and so definitely postwar and American with all that fabric and brightness that I felt brave and empowered in them.

I chose the orange dress for the dinner party and went off with Antonio under the medieval porticos of his Via Santa Lucia, a venerable street with humble fruit stands and dark stores that ran from one of the old city gates to the piazza at Ponte degli Angeli, the bridge of angels, over the river Retrone. Along the way was the old building where Antonio's great grandmother Catin had lived. The street had once been fine, but was now rundown.

The Z——s lived in the center of town in one of the palaces fronting on the Corso. Arrived there, I found everyone in uniform: the women wore black, well-cut dresses and strings of pearls; the men were in grey with striped ties. I began to feel not so brave, but rather like a great orange pumpkin-bumpkin in that staid company, and thrust my hands into the comforting security of my deep pockets. Antonio noticed not a thing, carried away as he always was with the dazzle of his talk and storytelling and his unswerving conviction that anything I did or wore was wonderful. Shades of my old Convent School, I thought to myself: everyone else in uniform and me the standout misfit.

I sat in a circle of ladies in black. Not the dowdy black of those Italian American women on the north side of Syracuse, before whom I used to cringe, feeling the shame of association with such backward people. My surname marked me, as theirs did them, Italian American in a discriminatory time. There was discrimination even in Italy, since everyone knew that most Italian Americans were descended from southern immigrants, the *terroni* of Calabria, Naples, or Sicily. And the north was different. Hadn't Antonio, jesting, told me that for him, a northener, to marry someone of the south there had to have been the purifying influence of my being a third-generation American? But the jest held an ineluctable truth.

The black dress of the Vicenza women was not that of my grandmother in her kitchen, stirring soup. The Vicenza uniform was the elegant "indispensable little black dress" of *Vogue* and *Harper's Bazaar* which my mother subscribed to and I perused. I had in fact entered the *Vogue* Prix de Paris contest in my senior year in college. I did have a sense of style and what was right; I was class conscious. I did want to evolve and compete for a job on a fashion magazine.

Through all these years I've still kept copies of the four Prix "quizzes," so-called, which I had to complete. Each quiz had two questions, one on fashion and one on a general topic. Asked, in the first fashion question, to select a wardrobe, I had responded that I wore "simple, classic lines rather than extreme styles." I chose from *Vogue*'s pages a black suit and a black dress writing, "I wear a lot of youthful black because it is flattering to my type . . ."

So what revolution in my thinking had taken place from my college days to my flamboyant appearance three years later at the Z——s dinner party?

Not only had I known what apparel was right for the occasion, I had been reinforced in the ways of *una vera signora* (a true lady) by Antonio's relative, Lisetta, who often visited his mother's home in Vicenza as if on a spa vacation.

Lisetta, a woman of indeterminable age, was the object of disapproval and consternation in the family (and probably not a little envy, as well) for her free ways and *savoir vivre*. Lisetta, with her dyed coppery-orange hair that almost matched my Claire McCardell dress, her blue eyes and perfect white skin, was the eccentric maverick in the Vicenza milieu. She resided in hotels, for one thing. Had never had a home or a husband—only a lover named Cesare who had deserted his family for her, living off her money until he finally deserted her, too, leaving Lisetta with dozens of his custom-made, monogrammed silk shirts which she promptly hocked.

"She's crazy, unbalanced, mad enough to be committed," Antonio's sister would say of Lisetta. "She's squandered her money in lawsuits and has the illusion of being a clever woman of the world. Between doctors and lawyers, she's spent everything she ever had. Not to mention, of course, what Cesare cost her!"

I loved Lisetta's visits. She brought something zany into the household and she was filled with lore and advice. We were friends from the very beginning, and later she told me that the reason we struck it off so well was that we were both cosmopolitan. For if I had come from America, she had once been to Munich with Cesare and that meant we were both degrees removed from provincialism.

I would sit with Lisetta in the kitchen during her visit, having my morning coffee while she blanched her fine smooth hands in lemon juice and imparted the rules of being *una vera signora*. Quite emphatically she decreed that a real lady wore only black, with pearls or diamonds after five in the afternoon. "And at no time, day or night, should a lady wear a cameo—it's too Neopolitan." Then, quite blithely, she disregarded the rules and wore her own eccentric concoctions at whatever time she pleased.

Still, why did I go to an evening dinner party with important people in my husband's hometown wearing the wrong outfit? And why did Antonio not object? Had my long-standing identity conflict asserted itself beyond my control? I must have unconsciously wanted to go as the Outsider, the shocker of the bourgeoisie, the poet's wife, the budding writer. There was something superbly insouciant about my billowing, voluminous Claire McCardell design in addition to its orangey bright glow in that grey Vicenza chill. It was very American, and that's what I was feeling. I could have written the *Vogue* copy for that dress: ". . . a wrapped collar can add personality since such a neckline is changeable according to who wears it . . . an animating factor, a final gesture akin to the flourish of an artist's signature."

Why wouldn't I have chosen my Claire McCardell ready-to-wear over any safe and sure little black dress from a Vicenza seamstress!

It was part of my youthful rebellion. I had gone to Europe in the first place, rather than to New York to be a secretary in a publishing firm—the aspiration of almost everyone else in my group.

Either that, or they got married and settled down in Syracuse to what I considered the most humdrum of lives. I wanted none of that, and when I was given a letter of introduction to a poet named Antonio Barolini, I felt I was entering a special world that I would never have accessed staying home in Syracuse and continuing in my copywriting job at Edwards Department Store.

I aspired to know poets and artists and to dine in society. Perhaps I wanted too much and got confused. The wearing of that orange dress was not so much my declaration of independence as the signal of a deeply unresolved conflict about who I was and where I belonged.

That Vicenza evening at the Z——s', I don't remember what I said or to whom as we sat in a circle in the salon before dinner, sipping an aperitif and having a roasted almond or two. The Z——s were quite formal and stuffy. Just as—I knew from my reading of nineteenth-century English novels—always happened to ordinary families when they are suddenly enriched and are edging into the realm of the elite. They become correct and stiff, not at ease like the *decaduti* I met, the highborn who have fallen on hard times through two crushing world wars that all but leveled them. I was thinking of Antonio's several-times-removed cousin, *contessina* Nini Piovene (still called with the childhood diminutive for *contessa* because she had never married). Then well into middle age, Nini was the only one of her family left in Vicenza. She lived in the head gardener's quarters behind the grand palazzo whose rooms had been turned into rentable apartments. She lived among heaps of furniture taken from the palazzo and when we entered her place it looked like a thrift shop from home. She was cordial and at her ease, with no laments for her diminished fortunes. She was interested in Antonio's work and in me, his American bride.

"I will give you a wedding gift," she announced grandly. "Look around at what I have here and I will sell very reasonably, as my gift to you, whatever you choose."

I was taken aback: buy my own wedding gift? But Antonio registered no surprise.

"Nini, are you sure?" he asked. "After all, you may one day go back to the palazzo and you will want your things."

"I wouldn't go back to that drafty old place, even if I could. What would I do in that great heap, rattling around! Other times! Now I live here." She was an imperious and striking woman, her head wrapped in a turban and her words emphasized by taps of her cane on the floor.

I adjusted from my initial surprise and quite contentedly picked out four graceful, rounded-back Empire chairs to go with a dining table from Antonio's mother.

"A fine choice," said Nini, "you can have the lot for 20,000 lire." Even in those days when the lire was nowhere near as inflated as later, that was a bargain, and since the chairs are still with me I have many times thought what a real gift Nini gave us, even though they have cost their price several times over in restoration. They are delicate pieces, already 150 years old when we bought them a half-century ago. They cannot tolerate being tilted on their back legs as my six-foot-tall son-in-law would do, or bear excessive weight or leaning on. They are fragile but beautiful, and I infrequently use them at the table. Now they are side chairs and perennial, daily reminders of gallant *contessina* Nini who died long ago, indomitable, unstiffened by convention, code, or remorse.

Not so the Z——s, stiff as ramrods, so new and precariously unfamiliar was their toe-hold on society. The night of their dinner party we were ushered from the salon into a stately dining room where a huge oval table sat some twenty of us. Antonio was placed a good distance from me and went on talking animatedly, quite unconcerned about my being marooned far away from him.

As the new bride, I was served first with a fine consomme by a *maggiordomo* who wore white gloves. That was the easy part. The table was elaborately set with tableware that promised a succession of courses, and after the broth I was approached by the butler, proffering a silver platter on which two entire fish reposed. I looked at them; I looked down the table to Antonio, but he had his head turned, still talking away to the person on his left. He was no help.

I recalled that fish had already played an ominous role in my new life at the wedding dinner hosted at my sister-in-law's for an intimate group. The fish course, a lovely large poached sea bass adorned with freshly made mayonnaise and decorative designs on a bed of vegetables, suddenly became suspect. "*Mah! Sa di fango,*" said my sister-in-law as she tried her serving and pronounced that it tasted of mud. The fish was removed and dumped, though I hadn't detected anything wrong and always thought it a dreadful waste, even bad form on my sister-in-law's part to have made such a depressing statement on such an occasion.

What was I to do at the Z——s? I weighed the situation. Certainly at such an elaborate dinner with so many present there would be a procession of other white-gloved servers with more platters of fish. Reassured, I served myself one of the two fish on the platter. And then I watched, rigid with horror as the others at table each cut themselves a token piece of the remaining fish.

It was a defining moment of cultural shock. What was I doing there? I was an American young woman of Italian background through my second-generation parents, themselves the children of immigrant Italian parents who had not practiced table niceties in their struggle for survival. I was the first of my family to have a college education. I had grown up in a two-family house until the time when, during the war, my father's produce business had flourished and he had moved us to a picturesque fieldstone house on Syracuse's best street across from the Catholic bishop's mansion. I had gone to Wells College where Frances Folsom, our most famous alum, had been courted by President Grover Cleveland, whom she had married in the White House. I had acquired certain notions of gentility, but obviously not enough to help me through the Z——s' dinner party.

Finally, Antonio looked up and saw what had happened. Of the two fish that were to be divided among twenty diners, I had taken one for myself. He made a light remark regretting that he could not increase the remaining fish as had once been done for a hungry crowd in Galilee. The company politely tittered, but I was left marooned with my fish, mentally absenting myself from everyone. Where did I fit? Certainly not in the conventional routine of a provincial Italian town. Did there flit through my mind the place card written for me at Wells' freshman banquet? "Someday I shall find my place in the world,"—some ironic sophomore had prophesized for me.

I must have gotten through the rest of the dinner, but I don't remember anything after the fish. We must have left the table and sat again in a circle in the salon passing chocolates around because that's what was done at Italian dinner parties at that time. But I don't remember.

And yet there's something more to that evening—there was the layer of rigid snobbery that had left me to fend for myself. Everyone so wrapped up in a notion of correctness that not one of them could laugh at my gaffe and help rescue me from my predicament. Why hadn't someone stopped the absurdity of my taking a whole fish? Couldn't the person on my left or right, either one of those gentlemen, have spoken to the butler and righted the situation?

And the Z—— matriarch, a formidable lady of stern face and iron-grey hair who sat motionless and expressionless at the opposite end of the table from me, why didn't she call out gaily, as *contessina* Nini might have, "*Cara mia!* We've made things too difficult for you! Giuseppe, scoop that fish from the *signora's* dish and help her to a proper portion."

It reminded me of my college Spanish class where we were taught by a relentless woman professor to lisp our *c*'s in the Castillian manner because the Spanish king, Felipe II, was a lisper and so the whole silly court, and then the whole country, followed suit and lisped their *c*'s in order to pretend he had no impairment.

It was the same that evening when everyone at the table pretended nothing was wrong. My social error was passed over in the deep collusion of silence. And I say now, a half-century later, that it was my hosts who should have rescued me! Now I see the correct response would have been a laugh and a reprieve. And I would have been off the hook for taking a whole fish. Or were they as uncertain of themselves as I was?

Perhaps we were all in that human comedy together, bumbling through the imbroglio as best we could, the Z——s in their uniforms of advancement, me in my aspiring orange. There we were in the postwar brave new world, trying to find our places.

I have been back to Vicenza many times since I first arrived as a bride. I went back to accompany my deceased husband's ashes for burial in the crypt of the Vicenza cemetery reserved for the city's distinguished citizens. I have seen Via Santa Lucia rise from its decrepit postwar state to its recent regentrification as a residential street for young business and professional people. And on the facade of the old palace where I had come as a bride there is a plaque that states that Antonio Barolini once lived there and there wrote "exquisite images of his poet's art."

I, too, his American wife, lived there with our first child, but we are not recorded and chiseled in stone. For the marker on that street belongs to his city's memory of Antonio, and gone, far gone and obliterated, is any recollection of the gauche outsider bride in the orange dress who helped herself to one whole fish at the Z——s' dinner party and was briefly (and uniquely in her life) the talk of the town.

Montale and Mosca in a Train

Growing up I was given Nancy Drew books for my birthday, and other reading came from my visits to the Eastwood branch of the Syracuse Public Library. The first book purchase at a bookstore I ever made for myself was T. S. Eliot's *Four Quartets*. Perhaps from my childhood readings in *My Bookhouse* and Longfellow's *Collected Poems* I had begun to value poetry. When my mother chided me in my high school years for not being popular and going out on dates, I responded, "Popular! Who cares about popular! I'm going to marry a poet . . . be a poet!" It was a wild assertion. For what did I know about poets? Eliot himself was said to have remarked of poetry that it was a superior amusement. Was that all? Or was a poet some superior being who saw into things and could render profundities in memorable and moving language?

I can smile now at my youthful quest, but it was prophetic. After college I attended a summer course in contemporary English poetry at the University of London, a stop en route to my real destination, Italy. Not knowing the language, or anyone in Italy to help me find sources for a series of articles I was writing for my hometown paper, it was just luck that a fellow student in London wrote me a letter of introduction to an Italian journalist in Milan who might help me. I met the journalist. He was also a poet. Reader, I married him.

I was ingenuous enough at the time to be surprised that a journalist could also be a poet. American poets all seemed to be in the English departments of colleges, or living like hermits in the boondocks. Eventually in Italy, where all writers seemed to have begun as poets, I came to my own definition: poetry was for me an emboldened shorthand of the spirit.

I had arrived in Europe years before mass tourism and study programs abroad abounded. It was perhaps the last of the old Europe, still in its post–World War II burst of liberation and creativity before the advent of the Iron Curtain and dominant American influences.

So there I am, a young American bride with an older Italian husband, balding, doting, and fussy in bachelor-like ways. He is Antonio, of Venetian family but working in Milan since the end of the war; he knows everyone in literary circles in Italy. With Antonio's journalist's pass allowing us generous discounts on train travel, we are in a first-class train compartment en route to Venice. Our travel companions are poet Eugenio Montale who is also a journalist writing the cultural columns, the *elzeviri*, for the illustrious third page of Italy's premier paper, *Il Corriere della Sera*. Were we going to Venice's Art Biennale? Or was that the time that Montale, as music critic, covered the world premiere in Venice of Stravinsky's opera, *The Rake's Progress*, with book by W. H. Auden? I no longer remember.

In prewar years, Antonio, an aspiring poet younger than Montale, had first sought him out when Montale was living in Florence and part of a literary group there that met at the Caffè Giubbe Rosse in Piazza della Repubblica. In Italy's postwar literary exuberance, Antonio had cofounded and edited a literary review called *Le Tre Venezie*, which published some of Montale's new work. I have among Antonio's papers the typed page of a poem Montale sent in, "L'ombra di magnolia," which carries in Antonio's hand the seventeen changes where he crossed out words and wrote in changes. Montale accepted them and they were carried forward into his next volume of poetry, *La Bufera*, containing most of the *Finisterre* poems. Montale was very fond of

Antonio and gave him the original typescript of *Finisterre* written during the war years and smuggled to Switzerland by a friend where it was first published in 1943. Montale's gift was inscribed on the cover page, "To Antonio with great affection and gratitude, Eusebio, 1948."

In the late 1940s both Antonio and Montale were working in Milan and met often. Eventually we departed for the United States when Antonio was named the American correspondent for *La Stampa* and he and Montale kept in touch by letter. Montale's review of Antonio's new book appeared in *Il Corriere della Sera* under the heading, "A Poet Dispersed among Men," with the opening line, "Barolini was not born modern, this is known and says nothing. More interesting, instead, is to note that he hasn't lifted a finger to become so." The review is long and favorable. It may have been Antonio's intense humanity and what Montale called his Venetian gift of gab that attracted the older man, so much more bleak and brooding in his world view. Montale had what critic Rebecca West has identified so accurately as both literary and personal hermeticism. Still he had once stated in an interview, "Some say that poets are crazy, but I say it's the non-poets. . . ."

On the train with Montale is his companion, Drusilla Tanzi Marangoni, who is known by his name for her, Mosca, which means fly. Sometimes, his address is elaborated to *mosca infernale*, "hellish fly." Mosca has told me she loathes her given name; but I don't—it reminds me of a well-loved tale from my childhood about a doll named Drusilla and it has for me, enchanted by all things Italian, echoes of ancient Rome.

Eugenio Montale is known to his intimates as Eusebio (a name with resonance of early church fathers) and is already a distinguished poet although it will be almost another quarter century before he receives the Nobel Prize for literature. He is a portly man with a soft, sagging face and eyes bulging from the fleshy mass. I do not think he is attractive and his table manners are even less so: he ducks his head almost into his plate and wolfs his food. He does not make conversation at the table. Antonio has mentioned that his table manners are said to have kept him from an ambassadorship. Montale is the age of my father and this erects a barrier of respect and awe between us. In the train compartment, where he smokes, he notes aloud my silence.

"She is serene," says Antonio rather proudly.

"In time she will find her tongue," says Montale prophetically.

On this occasion he is also very entertaining. He tells the story of how he assisted at the emergence of the Sicilian poet Lucio Piccolo. It seems that one day there arrived in Montale's mail a privately published little volume of poetry printed on cheap paper and mailed from Sicily to Milan with only a 35-lire stamp so that another 180 lire was due and had to be paid by Montale, the recipient. The inauspicious little volume was titled *Nine Lyrics* and in an attached note the author introduced himself simply as a Sicilian dedicated to put into poetry the baroque world of Sicily that now teetered on extinction. His little book was not in commerce. He excused himself for the intrusion. Such books, Montale says, arrive to him by the hundreds each year and form piles and mounds on his library table until Gina the housekeeper silently disposes of them. But Piccolo's little book did not get discarded.

"Perhaps," Montale tells us, "I wanted to see if it were worth the extra postage I had to pay for it."

It overwhelmingly was. So much so that Montale presented the book, which he assumed was the work of a young man on his first publishing venture and without contacts in the literary world, at that summer's Literary Award event at the fashionable watering spa of San Pellegrino in Lombardy. The theme that year was "A Meeting between Generations," in which some of Italy's most important and well-established older writers, like Montale, would each present a "new hope" of the younger generation. So what was his surprise to see that the unknown Sicilian who had sent him the typographically modest volume was not a friendless young man but a fifty-three-year-old aristocrat, the Baron Piccolo, who was accompanied to the spa event by his cousin, Prince Giuseppe Tomasi di Lampedusa, who was to become famous as the author of *The Leopard*. They were, Montale says, two elderly provincials with the pallor of indoor recluses, wearing dark suits of old-fashioned cut and accompanied by a valet.

And Montale, with his rapid talk and cigarette smoking, smiles and says that he is not an emotive man, but even he had his moment of astonishment and double take at the encounter: his protege was a mature man of means who read Wittgenstein and Greek tragedy in the original, had carried on a correspondence with Yeats, and had an imposing musical background. This was the presumed novice that he was to hold at baptism into the Italian literary world!

And so, as it goes, the rest is history. Montale's sponsorship made Lucio Piccolo known, his complete oeuvre of thirty-six poems, *Canti Barocchi*, was published to acclaim in Italy and then translated into English.

I was introduced to Montale's poetry by Antonio as I was learning Italian: the glorious poems "I Limoni," "Portovenere," "La Casa dei Doganieri," "L'anguilla," "L'ombra della magnolia," and so many more. Many poems were dedicated to Mosca whom Montale met in Florence when he was director of the Vieusseux Library there and his first collection of poetry, *Ossi di seppia*, had already been published. Mosca was at that time married to Signor Marangoni and had a son, whom she left for the poet. It's a romantic story of their youth and I believed in it. Perhaps at that time, besides Mosca's belief in Montale's poetry and her independent income, she had also beauty. In any case her devotion and dedication proved pivotal to the poet for it was said that Mosca's connections got him noticed. It seemed to me good that they met and became joined for he is a true poet and she was his helpmate.

But now in the compartment of the *rapido* going from Milan to Venice, Mosca is an aging woman wearing thick bifocal glasses and too much makeup.

"You look like a clown," Montale tells her sharply. She has two big spots of rouge on her cheeks. She takes out a compact and dabs some powder on her face.

I am uncomfortable on many levels. I do not yet know enough Italian to engage in intricate conversation; I can follow what's said and make simple remarks but I cannot say to Montale in any depth how much his poetry means to me and how I would like someday to translate some of it. But I hear and understand his unkind jabbing at Mosca and it bothers me.

How can so fine a poet say those things? Don't finer feelings make a finer person? Out of the blue I think of my father. Forcing silence on the rest of us, he ate in silence making exceptions only for sarcastic remarks to my mother about the food if it displeased him. His sarcasm was also aimed at me as I was growing up overweight, a dumpy little girl. It made me want to starve myself and so I did: in my adolescence, I stopped eating and no one seemed to notice until I was not only underweight (no one used the term anorexic at that time) but also anemic, and had to be given horrible liver shots under a doctor's care.

But my father's anger originated in his hard life—he had not been able even to finish high school; he had had to work from childhood and could not be expected to have the sensibility and learning of a poet even though there were certain lines of Sir Walter Scott memorized in his early school days that he liked to repeat when he had had a few drinks: "Breathes there the man with soul so dead / Who never to himself hath said / This is my own, my native land!" He worked hard as head of a wholesale produce business that required his rising early in the dark of morning and going to the market while the rest of us slept. He brought home the wherewithal that gave us our advantages and upward mobility and I learned from my mother that that was what was important—not his temper. She accepted everything in exchange for being taken care of. It was what women did then.

What I am saying is how simple a person I was: poets acted one way, men at the market another. And then in an Italian train compartment I learn how more complex and unexpected life is than the notions formed in my upstate New York, ordinary childhood.

How did I get to be a literalist?—someone who thought poets should fit an uplifted notion of them? Perhaps it was due to a certain insecurity and unease I have always felt—a veritable homesickness—because I did not feel at home even in the very place that was my home, where I might have felt secure and protected.

In the train I am more upset by Montale's badinage than either Antonio or Mosca is. When I ask Antonio later why Montale spoke like that to her, Antonio, who is kind-hearted and affable, says it is his kind of teasing affection for her. I do not think so. I think it is the reverse of the love he once had for her showing its dark side because they are now married and he is tied to her and she is aging and ugly.

Mosca died in 1963. In 1966 Montale inscribed "To Helen and Antonio Barolini a remembrance of dear Mosca and of Eusebio," a privately printed copy of his *Xenia* poems, one of fifty published in remembrance of Mosca. The dedication was "To My Wife." I asked his permission to translate some of the poems, he gave it, and in 1967 my *Xenia* translations were the first to appear in an American publication (but never mentioned in the lists of Montale translations by those in the academic or publishing world who took over the Montale opus). My *Xenia* translations were published in the *Quarterly Review of Literature* and later reprinted in

Theodore & Renée Weiss's *Thirtieth Anniversary Poetry Retrospective* where a blurb newly introduced me as a writer and a translator of Italian authors.

And in the *Xenia* poems the use of the name "Mosca" makes it seem indubitably linked to the insect: "Sans glasses / sans antennae / a poor little fly whose wings / existed only in fantasy." But the word "fantasy" puts the allusion in doubt.

Now the others of this story have long been dead—Mosca, Antonio, and Montale. And the photo of Montale that appears on the brochure I receive from the Centro Internazionale Eugenio Montale features on its cover a smiling, affable, benign Montale with his hand raised as if in greeting. And I wonder about the naming of "Mosca." Was she capriciously identified with the insect, or did that name have another reference which has so long been masked by the literal translation of *mosca* to fly?

And what if there were a connection to the Mosca in Dante's *Divine Comedy*? Having been allowed to audit the graduate classes on the *Commedia* conducted by my eldest daughter, a professor of Italian literature at Columbia University, I noted a certain Mosca first mentioned in Canto 6 of the *Inferno* when Dante asks his guide if some notable Florentines, including Mosca, are in Heaven or Hell. In deepest Hell, is the answer and thus the thirteenth-century Mosca reappears in Canto 28, the eighth ring of Hell where the makers of discord are punished. This Mosca was a Florentine nobleman who, in political life, was responsible for divisions that led to long-lasting feuds among the Guelfs and the Ghibellines, and eventually, the extinction of families. It was Mosca, as part of a group that wanted to avenge an insult to their family and were planning some kind of punishment to the perpetrator, who made it a death sentence with his famous remark, "*Cosa fatta capo ha.*" In other words, do it to make an end of it.

Was Montale's naming of his lifetime companion "Mosca" tied to that saying, implying that by her leaving her husband, she took a step that was decisive and would not be undone? In speaking of her as *Mosca infernale*, did he refer, then, not to a bothersome fly, but to that discordant citizen of Florence sent to Hell for doing something drastic, knowing there was no turning back? It is too late to know, and yet to me it suddenly made sense and certainly dignified Montale's partner from pest to person of destiny.

Still with me, always visible in the morning when I awaken, and the last thing I see at night when I turn out the light in my bedroom, is the pastel drawing of a vase of flowers dated 1955 that Montale gave me so long ago. The pastel is very tenuous and faint, barely visible—a contrast to his poetry as well as to his deep bass voice. It speaks of something delicate and sensitive in him, something that offsets his mocking of Mosca; for he was, after all, with her to the last and gave her continuous life in his touching verses to her. And that's how I remember them.

As I keep remembering lines from his "Lemon Trees" (*I limoni*) that so directly sing the triumph of sunlight, of hope over doubt, of the heart's resurgence:

> Then one day through a half-shut gate
> leading to courtyard foliage
> yellow lemons bare themselves to us
> and the icy heart just melts
> and in our breasts burst forth
> their songs,
> golden trumpets of high sun.

Sicily, Light and Dark

On a school vacation when we were living in Rome, my husband and I decided to take our children to Taormina in Sicily for Easter. High above the sea that laps on Sicilian shores, Taormina is one of earth's beauty spots; as scenery it is superb, but as a town it is, alas, an artifice, a package showpiece more than a living place.

If, as my first boss once confided to me, position in life is everything, then Taormina has it. The town sits perfectly terraced and gardened on Mt. Tauro on the eastern coast of Sicily, facing the Ionian Sea with Mt. Etna in grand view to the south. One can't cavil with paradise. Nor can one visit unmoved the ruins of Taormina's Greek amphitheater so perfectly set between mountain and sea, so poignant in ruin, so overrun with the prolific wildflowers and sunshine of Italy. But the price for such beauty is high. Taormina is overrun with tourists and has lost her identity to them. They come in huge busloads from the North countries clogging the narrow streets; they spill out into piazzas, street caffes, the beaches, the shops, the mountain paths.

But how could Taormina be anything but despoiled? The economic advantage is too clear. No other town in Sicily is so pretty and clean and amenable to tourist sensibilities. In Taormina there is no dirt or poverty, nor are there begging children with eyes to pierce into your heart and disturb your peace. Instead, the shop windows beckon with the icons of a non-town—Japanese camera supplies, American cosmetics and canned corn niblets, English tea biscuits, German girlie magazines, and the whole gamut of international stylized junk made to the standards of that crass entity known as the tourist trade.

Souvenirs exploit indigenous Sicilian folk art on blouses and hats and baskets embroidered with the donkey cart motif; ceramics are full of it. Fake bits of the *carro siciliano* are piled on sidewalks together with dubious Sicilian puppets and spurious bits of antiquity. Postcards are there by the thousands, even those notorious ones catering to special tastes which feature nude youths of Taormina wreathed in laurel and assuming classical poses for the delight of the foreigners who began collecting them in the Victorian era. Each little shop is the same as the next. And they all spill out into the Corso, the town's one through street, where from morning to night the tourists file past. The women seem to dress mostly in ugly stretch pants with foot straps and carry folk-art handbags; men wear sunglasses and shoulder-strap cameras.

I've seen non-towns before—they're Carmel, Hyannis, Taos, and all those other little communities that live, like something spoiling, by attracting hordes of fly-tourists to buzz around crazily in a semblance of life and activity, to feed greedily on them, and then to leave. The non-towns are completely detached from their environments; they are groomed and swept to keep up appearances and are conspicuously full of beguilements for tourist money.

Signs and notices in Taormina are in English, German, French, and Italian—although sometimes there is no Italian. I hear it used so seldom that I begin to wonder what the real inhabitants speak. Have they perhaps lost their native tongue, possessing now only a melange of useful tourist phrases?

Bars and caffes and restaurants feature what they think the foreigners will like—hamburgers, English tea, and those ubiquitous ice cream products made in Milan after Good Humor models. The native dishes (like the *cassatta siciliana*, queen of all frozen desserts) seen to have disappeared. When I stopped in a bakery to ask for the traditional Easter sweet, *torta di ricotta*, I was told there is so little request that it was only made on special order.

"But why, it's so Sicilian!" I said, unwilling to believe that during Easter week in Sicily I couldn't get something so dear to custom that it still appears on the Easter tables of Sicilians who have already lived three generations in, let's say, Syracuse, New York.

"The foreigners don't like it," said the baker with unconcern. "This is what they like." He pointed to the little almond paste cookies that ladies all over the world have with their tea.

We actually knew in advance it would be so. When we told friends in Rome we were going to Taormina for Easter vacation, they groaned and said, "Why, do you want to spend it with Germans?" Not particularly, perhaps, but with only a few free days, there was no time to find unspoiled, unvisited places. Besides, to be unspoiled would mean no facilities. For our brief time we wanted spring flowers, a pleasant pensione, and a beach for sunbathing. But then so did everyone else. And they were all in Taormina.

Not all places become non-towns. The great places survive despite the tourist hordes because of their art treasures, their strong identities, and the vitality of their people—Venice, Paris, Santa Fe: there are plenty of them. It's the smaller places which are more vulnerable: those that offer, mainly, splendid natural settings and sweet climates. Those that have become centers for foreign resident colonies of writers and artists and their well-off patrons.

The strange thing, however, is that D. H. Lawrence, indisputably a first-rater, had a penchant for such locales—he lived in at least two, Taormina and Taos. But then he lived everywhere and nowhere, a restless wayfarer always on the move, always pushing on to new paradises with Frieda in immediate tow and assorted coteries of handmaidens always showing up afterward at each of his successive tries at settlement.

In Taormina the Lawrences lived at Villa Fontana Vecchia, a nice big house of large rooms and pleasant terraces set in the green of almond trees on a steep slope above the sea; there was in the villa even the kind of kitchen that Frieda could enjoy—a light-filled, handy, blue one built by Dutch owners and, outside, an abundant fruit and vegetable garden. There Frieda, hausfrau wherever she lighted, even in the Garden of Eden, baked their breads, made their jams, picked *nespoli* from the laden trees, and washed down the pretty blue tile floors. And Lorenzo, as she called him in their Italian period, padded about barefoot in his pajamas, wrote prodigiously, sat for sketches, walked up and down the mountain paths to bathe in the sea, visited the Duke of Bronte on his estate just under Etna (and found him to be a descendant of the first Duke, the English naval hero, Lord Nelson), condescended to be served teas and dinners by the resident English colony whom he mostly despised, read Verga, and declined to contribute toward the erecting of an English church in Taormina.

They loved the town at first. Then, after a few months, despite the low rent, the heady views and delicious sea-winds, Lawrence was already writing to discourage his friends from ever thinking of living in Sicily; and though he and Frieda kept the house in Taormina for two years, this period was broken by many lengthy side trips and periodical complaints in his letters about the life-lessness of the South.

Aside from Lawrence's fundamental restlessness, which kept him permanently unsettled, perhaps it was also the dissatisfaction with perfection that made him leave Taormina. Something there is, certainly, in the southern air which makes a scrupulous Nordic temperament uneasy. Goethe noted it too, even though he recalled with nostalgia, years after his Sicilian trip, that perfect interlude of peace when he sat in an orange grove just out of Taormina, lost in fancy as he gazed at the sea below, and mused on a plot for the dramatization of the story of Nausicaä. Nausicaä, daughter of an island king, enamored of Ulysses—perhaps she was Sicilian, too, as so many mythological figures were. Goethe was to recall from his German home the sublimity of that southern scenery and classic soil which seemed to exact some noble work from him. And yet, pleasant as it might have seemed to him to linger in "this school for easy, happy living," his northern sense of propriety would not permit it. Even so today, the busloads of Germans (read also, Swedes, Angles, Americans) come and go and, though some tarry in Taormina, the sterner spirits, those who have work to do and consciences to answer to, inevitably push on. For Taormina is simply not real; it is as Lawrence described it, a parterre—not nature, but an artfully composed garden bed: "the languors and lilies of virtue here very stiff and prickly, the roses and rapture of vice a little weedy and ill developed."

Taormina has found its raison d'etre in becoming what the foreign busloads want it to be. An American resident of Taormina with whom we have an apératif in the piazza tells us of being summoned, along with all other members of the resident foreign colony, to a town meeting in order to make suggestions as to what else might be done to make Taormina even more attractive to visitors. And I wonder aloud why no one has suggested that, bother the tourists, Taormina needs a high school for her own children so they needn't rise at dawn and take a train back and forth to Catania if they are to continue their schooling past the elementary grades.

But foreign interests must be cultivated. Thus the abundance of nightclubs and beachboys to cater to visiting blondes. Thus the plethora of local agencies which provide excursions to Etna, to nearby grottoes, to waterfalls, to any place that can be photographed by the camera crowd. Thus the ugly art shows in the thirteenth-century Parliament House which point out perhaps better than anything else what the decadence of taste is bound to be in a non-town. Everything is arty; but there is no art.

In this unreal town the Public Gardens are the epitome of unreality. They have formal, beautiful flower beds laid out impeccably, a caged peacock in a cage too small for him to unfold his tail, weirdly constructed grotesqueries of ramps and stairways that lead nowhere, and a setting of boulders made to resemble (but why?) a miniature Stonehenge. Everything is still, and the town fathers must have decided that tourists like it that way. The ice cream vendors and balloon men that can be found in any other public park of Italy are prohibited here. So there are no children at play, the place is quiet, and a tourist can sit and read in peace his foreign newspaper.

We met the broad and beaming Germans everywhere up and down the mountain on which Taormina sits. They are on the walks down to the sea; they are on the climb to the summit above Taormina where the remains of a medieval fortress still stand. Once in a while on these walks we hear an English or French phrase, and the novelty of it only emphasizes how much German is in the air. Down in the town, at a bookstore, I remark on this. "*Si, signora*," says the vendor, "Easter is the German time; if you want to hear English, you come in January; for French, July and August. And if you want to hear us in Taormina speaking Italian, come in November—then no one is here." But yes, someone was there in November the year my husband and I honeymooned there. It was Truman Capote sitting in Caffe Nuovo having a drink. We had come down from Milan and we and he were, perhaps, the only English-speaking people in town at the moment. We hadn't known our time was January.

One morning we rented a car, went down the mountain and drove to Schisò a few kilometers away on a road that kept the sea in sight. Outside the drab town, in an orange grove beside the sea are the remains of ancient Naxos, the first Greek colony in Sicily.

Remains? Barely. There is part of the stark black wall of lava blocks which surrounded the settlement; there is part of a kiln where the famous vases which now fill the museum at Syracuse were fired. And then there is the fragrance of orange blossoms, the slither of lizards in the warm sun, the profusion of flowers, the soft air that seems inevitably present in places of antiquity. There is nothing else to see, this is no Pompeii. And yet that stretch of wall is strangely moving; it was so very well cut from lava, the blocks so very well set without cement to form a defense that nevertheless stopped not a moment of Naxos's destruction. And now oranges grow where the Greeks colonized, and Sicily is visited by other waves of visitors. Perhaps we, too, in our way destroy places, leaving not orange groves along the sea in our wake but non-towns.

Following the shore we arrived at midday at a trattoria where we were told we could eat fish in the Sicilian manner—freshly caught and grilled with oil, lemon, parsley. We sat outdoors under a rude shelter hammered together from bits of boxes and rushes to shade us from the sun, and it was incomparably beautiful and pleasing: as always, flowers, sea, and blue sky. A woman came out from the kitchen, wiping her hands on her apron, and we discussed what she could give us: it was first, a plate of pasta with a sauce of fresh tomatoes and rosemary such as we hadn't once had in Toarmina—our pensione catered to the Swiss taste which meant thick cream soups—and then fish in the Sicilian manner, and last, the fruits of Sicily heaped in a basket on our table and looking like a Caravaggio still life.

We were served by eleven-year-old Alfio, the woman's son. When we asked why he was there and not in school he answered proudly, "The teacher suspended me for a week for fooling around with my friends, so I told her *ciao* for good. They won't be seeing me anymore at that school—at any school!" He is quick and bright and seems to be the whole force and spirit of that trattoria. We wonder if he hammered together the shelter, bargained with the fishermen for their catch, and told his mother what to charge.

Following lunch we continued on the sea road which would lead eventually to Catania and then Syracuse. But we weren't going that far, we were looking for the house by the medlar tree which gave the English title to Giovanni Verga's great novel about Sicilian life, *I Malavoglia*. So we stopped in Acitrezza and went to the main piazza of that old fishing village which spreads alongside a cove and there was a sight which knocked our eyes out: the rocks of the Cyclops were rising sheer out of the sea just as the giant Polyphemus was said to have hurled them in rage after the wily Ulysses who had blinded him and fled with his men. The sight is stupendous. The rocks are called the Faraglioni and in *The House by the Medlar Tree* the Malavoglia men are always sailing their fishing craft past them.

Acitrezza is not Taormina—it has the look of long-standing misery which seems the imprint of real Sicily. There we found a truer Sicily—squalid, but full of vitality. We thought of that somber Sicily whose people are sad within, depressed with the hopelessness of their history, that Sicily whose people live in the pages of her great writers: in Verga's stories and novels, in Pirandello's work, and in the contemporary novels of Brancati, Vittorini, and Sciascia. We thought of Vittorini's modern classic, *In Sicily*, a novel which portrays the soul of his country as emblematic of all humanity which suffers. It was while reading it that I understood what Goethe meant when he said, "To have seen Italy without having seen Sicily is not to have seen Italy at all, for Sicily is the clue to everything."

And it is Sicily's incredible light and dark—the white blare of sun on the sea against the dark, impenetrable mystery of the hovels where people live invisibly, the glare of light against those silent, black-garbed women of the South—the light and dark that was masterfully photographed as background in Antonioni's film *The Adventure*; it is this light and dark which is the plumb line of Pirandello's logic. One sees things instantly, logically, in Sicily with a Pirandellian non-emotionalism, without the shadings and nuances of a mainland chiaroscuro.

Acitrezza had this light and dark. But its inhabitants were not used to foreigners; they have not cultivated their town for the tourist trade. We asked a group of men in the piazza where we could find the house that served as the model of the one in Verga's book; among the men were the communal secretary and other leading citizens of Acitrezza. But they shrugged their shoulders as if at a joke. Verga once lived in Acitrezza, he is a giant among Sicilian writers, but no one knew anything at all about the house by the medlar tree. A young boy came up and said he could show us the place because some film people once passed through town and identified it.

The boy led us to an unsavory, narrow back alley where the look was indisputably that of Verga's story. He pointed out to us a poor, low stone house with a crooked wall surrounding a miniscule courtyard; a tin tub of weeds was perched cockeyed on the wall and in the courtyard sat two old women and a dignified old man weaving the rush baskets used by fishermen. Was this it? But there was no tree. We asked the old people. No, said one of the crones, there never was a medlar tree in the courtyard. Yes, said the other, it was here many years ago, in my mother's memory. A great argument ensued between the two women while the man sat there silent, weaving. It didn't matter. With or without the tree, we had the feel of the Verga story; we knew the Malavoglias could have lived there; we had the sense of Sicily.

A paradox: Lawrence, living in carefully cultivated Taormina, was attracted to Verga, the only Italian writer who interested him at all. And though Lawrence considered translating a waste of time, he was driven by his fascination with Verga to translate his stories and the novel *Don Gesualdo*. "It is pure Sicilian," Lawrence said of this book, "and you can see in it how heavy and black and hopeless are these Sicilians inside. Outside so beautiful. . . ."

In a way Taormina is to the whole of Sicily what *The Leopard* of Lampedusa is to the body of Sicilian literature. Both are beautiful and well-done and admirable; both are anomalies. Taormina does not represent the tormented island any more than *The Leopard* represents the mainstream of life there. The theme of *The Leopard* was prenoted a half-century earlier in Federico De Roberto's novel *The Viceroys*, and is captured in the character Tancredi's famous phrase, "If we want things to stay as they are, things will have to change." That is, if the privileged few—that stagnant group of cultivated, noble Sicilians so utterly removed from the misery of Sicilian life—want to remain privileged, they will have to feign change. And this has been Sicily's tragedy. *The Leopard* caught perfectly its own fragment of reality in Sicilian life, but it is the other great Sicilian writers who reach to the Sicilian soul.

We returned to Taormina, and for one hour the place seemed to be one with the rest of Sicily. It was Good Friday eve when a procession took place of the *Addolorata*, the sorrowing Mother of Jesus, seeking her crucified son. On both sides of the Corso, lines of black-robed women held candlelit lanterns which threw out a wavering red light. All stores and homes along the Corso were darkened; for once all tourist business had stopped.

In the street, a crowd thickened behind the procession. Between the lines of black women, little girls in white communion dresses and veils bore on silver platters the symbols of Christ's passion—the nails, the whip, the bag of silver pieces for which Judas had betrayed him. Then came the figures: Christ lay in a glass coffin carried on the shoulders of six young men of Taormina whose heads were ringed now, not by laurel for the porno postcards, but by thorns. A band followed and played Chopin's "Funeral March." Then came the figure of the sorrowing Mary, banked by hundreds of white Easter lilies, a cloth handkerchief in her plaster hands. It was very touching. For a bit Taormina's people had regained their town and made it theirs; it lived again in a pageant of death.

The next morning, in the bright sunlight, it was once more the poster place. It was as if, under the spell of tourism, Taormina is a Sleeping Beauty to be awakened only one hour each year for the Good Friday procession. But perhaps even an hour is something in the destiny of such places.

A Classical Excursion

When I learned that my liberal arts Wells College, founded for women in 1870 by Henry Wells of Wells Fargo fame, had, not long after celebrating its centennary, eliminated its Classics Department, I was staggered and saddened. How could an institution fostering the liberal arts eliminate the very bedrock of those arts, the Greek and Latin classics? After years of Latin at my convent school, I chose to continue it when I went on to Wells. Under the tutelage of gentle, erudite Miss Grether the two others and I who took her Latin courses read the elegiac poets of Rome, Cicero's elegant prose, and Horace's odes. It was the enlightenment moment of my education. It's what led me to Italy, and then to write.

When I first arrived in Italy and was headed for the University for Foreign Students in Perugia to study Italian, I traveled by bus from Rome and just past Spoleto the driver stopped along the dusty main road for an espresso break at Bar Clitunno. The name was immediately recognizable from the description by Propertius in one of his odes. And, in fact, across the road from the bar was the lovely little oasis surrounded by willows that the poet called Clitumnus. I went to see it, alone, while everyone else jammed the bar.

There it was, the sacred pool where, in the days of Rome's glory, cattle decked with floral wreaths were bathed before being sacrificed. The Clitunno springs spread out on the surrounding plains forming this limpid pool. So translucent and still, as Pliny the

Younger described it, "that you can count the coins that have been thrown into it and the pebbles glittering at the bottom." Even in antiquity, then, visitors threw coins in the fountain.

Later, much later, when I was married to Antonio, among the pleasures of living in Rome were our Sunday excursions to classical sites. One Sunday we set out for Horace's Sabine farm, the famed country place which the poet extols in his odes. The site is still there in the hills beyond Tivoli (the ancient Tibur whose metamorphosis from hard Latin into soft Italian was Tibur–Tibure–Tibor–Tivor–Tivoli) about forty miles from Rome, and the road we traveled, Via Tiburtina, follows the ancient route.

The way is dotted with remembrances: the sulfur baths whose waters were once piped into Nero's extravagant Golden House are still frequented, as in antiquity, by Romans seeking cures or simply a silkier skin; quarries still produce the Travertine blocks (*lapis Tiburtina*) that built the Colosseum and so much else; the ruins of circular tombs with their distinctive *opus reticulatum* brickwork can be glimpsed in the olive groves which bank the hill ascending to Tivoli.

We stopped in Tivoli, not for the usual visit to Villa d'Este built by a Renaissance cardinal and the destination of regular busloads of tourists, but for the views of ancient Tibur that Horace would have known, the places he frequented and the scenes he mentioned in his odes.

Skirting the town there is a road that circles the chasm where the river Aniene (the ancient Anio) drops in cascades (twice the fall of Niagara) over the wooded height on which Tivoli is built; there, says legend, in the caverns below the cascades dwelt the spirit of the river, the sibyl Ablunea whom Vergil has the king of Latium consult: "He sought a response . . . where Albunea's wood, among all woods supreme, echoes to a holy spring. . . ." The ancient Sibyl has long departed from Tivoli and her pagan memory is exorcised with a commonplace arch near the view of the falls inscribed "Ave Maria . . . . ," etc. For a small sum you can take a walk down a steep sign-marked path to the site of a cavern beneath the fall, but you'll get no prophetic response from it these days. In the cold of a New Hampshire winter I once came upon a sunny, romanticized view of the place done by the painter Lorrain and now hanging in the museum at Dartmouth College.

Across the gorge, on a terrace shared with the Ristorante della Sibilla where the Tivoli Rotary Club meets, are the remains of two classical temples. One, round and encircled with ten preserved Corinthian columns, might have been dedicated to the virginal Vesta and it owes its preservation to having been made into a Christian chapel for another virgin, namely, Mary; the other temple, less well-preserved and appearing more ancient, is the austere, rectangular shrine which was probably Sibyl's and owes what remains of it to having been dedicated to St. George until the end of the last century, when it was abandoned.

Although there is no certainty to whom the two Roman temples were dedicated in antiquity, there's no doubt as to who came in the modern era to see them. Cemented into the wall of the restaurant's foyer are numerous plaques—one for each illustrious visitor who came for the view and stayed to dine: Jerome Bonaparte, Prince Arthur of England, Grand Dukes and Grand Duchesses of Russia, Dutch royalty, and about every princeling in the numerous clan of the former Austrian-Hungarian Empire. It's strange to reflect that names of those Grand Tourists were there recorded for history while the deities of those two lovely temples are still matter for conjecture. To whom were they once dedicated? Along with the prophetic powers of the place, ancient inscriptions, too, have departed.

The best view of the Sibyl's wooded groves and leaping falls is from the other side of the gorge near the dwelling owned in recent times by an Englishman, replacing a former monastery which replaced a Roman villa. From there we get cascades, distant temples, and a gorge of spectacular greens—the silver green of olives, the blue-green of terraced and sprayed vines, the dark green flames of cypresses, somber hues of evergreens, the airy green of towering umbrella pines and the lacy chartreuse of spring when leaves are just coming into bud. And through them all is the shining, crystalline thread of the two-tiered falls and its muted sound as it plunges over rocks to repose in a light green pool.

Our view, we speculate, is from the supposed site of the villa of Horace's wealthy patron Maecenas, for its position, across the chasm from the falls and the Sibyl's temple, coincides with the remains of Roman brickwork and mosaics of a luxurious villa as does the poet's exhortation to his patron, "No more on Tibur's watery ways . . . gaze." Wealthy Romans had their summer villas at Tibur; Maecenas was both wealthy and a patron of the arts. That Horace was often his guest is easy to deduce for he speaks often of the delights of Tibur until, as he grew older and retired more and more completely to his farm, he excused himself in graceful odes to Maecenas for not visiting him more frequently.

Continuing along the same town-skirting road we come to a country church, Santa Maria Quintiliolo, and stop in the small square which fronts it. Adjoining the church and part of its property is a magnificent tract of olive trees extending over the still visible remains of another Roman villa. Tradition calls this the villa of Quintilius Varus who lived from 50 B.C. to A.D. 9 Quintilius Varus was the ill-fated general whom, in happy days, Horace called upon poetically to give no plant precedence at his Tibur villa over the sacred vine of Father Bacchus.

A man is washing his car in the church plaza; farther down the road six or seven cars are pulled into an olive grove where their owners scrub them down from the waters of a clothes-washing trough. Other cars are being washed at the Ave Maria arch. As we approach the grotto-like foundations of Varus's villa, we see yet another car in one of the grottoes, and beside it other debris of present, not ancient, civilization: plastic containers, tin cans, Coke bottles, papers. There is a double sadness—the sight of squalor at a lovely place, and the thought of Varus.

Sunt lacrimae rerum (There are tears in things), Vergil has Aeneas say when, at Carthage, he came upon painted scenes of the Fall of Troy, Priam's death, and other mournful reminders of events he has lived through. There are tears in things for, as associations, things have the power to reevoke memories of our personal past along with the collective human past. Everywhere human fate has the power to touch hearts: "I am human, nothing human is foreign to me," said Terence even before Vergil.

Remembrance of things past is strong in Tivoli—at least for us in the ruins of Quintilius Varus's villa. In this pleasant grove of centenarian olive trees and the soft murmuring of falling water, light breezes, sun, and peace, it is moving to think of that unlucky Varus whom Augustus Caesar sent off to the wild forests of the North in order to punish some of the Germanic tribes who had made incursions into Rome's empire. Poor Varus who left the cultivated company of Tibur and its exquisitely groomed slopes for the Teutonic thickets where, his three legions slaughtered and the Roman standards captured in an unparalleled catastrophe, nothing remained for him to do but to fall upon his own sword rather than into the hands of barbarians. It had been a massacre, an offense to the Roman eagle, an end to Augustus's plan of extending the empire further north. Suetonius recorded that for years after the disaster the Emperor would start from his sleep and cry out,"Varus, Varus, give me back my legions!"

Standing on the site of Varus's happy days and thinking of his end in the gloom of a northern forest among barbarians is Dantesque—*Nessun maggior dolore che ricordarsi del tempo felice nella miseria* (No greater sorrow than, in misfortune, to think back to happy times). So, perhaps Varus thought, recalling his home across the gorge from the sun-struck Sibyl's falls before he plunged on his sword and died his death of shame.

We went on to the country home that Maecenas, most enlightened of men whose very name identifies a wealthy patron, gave Horace to ensure his life and leisure in amenable surroundings conducive to poetry. Rome, the nerve center, the hub of the world, was too much for Horace; even pleasant Tibur was too much—all those villas on the slopes of Mt. Catilus meant no end of banquets and socializing. Horace loved conviviality but loved his personal freedom and solitude even more. He went further into the Sabine hills for his country retreat, into the Licenza river valley (Digentia, in antiquity) to a site just opposite the present town of Licenza.

It was always an unpopulated valley, but now it is almost devoid of trees as it was not in Horace's time or even as it appeared in eighteenth-century prints. A road marker announces the remains of Horace's villa and says that a foot journey (*viaggio pedonale*) of three minutes will take one to the site. The foot journey is up a steep cobblestone pathway. Along the way we met an old peasant couple, he leading a burro loaded with firewood, she with a huge pack of something (dandelion greens? acorns? wild asparagus?) on her head. We greeted each other, as is done in Italy, and in less than five minutes of encounter came to know that they live in Licenza, have nine children of whom the youngest is twenty-two and just home from military service, and though times are hard they were harder before.

Our rocky path is through a woody growth filled with the wild flowers of late March—violets, cyclamen, daisies, buttercups, primula, grape hyacinth. We wonder by what names Horace would have known them; he does not name them in his poetry as an English poet might. At the top of the path the bulldozers have been at work making a clearing for a car park and we thank our lucky stars that we got there in time before it's in use.

Even the caretaker is indignant. Not only a car park will be built but they will enlarge (and pave over?) the rough path and build a road the short distance up to the Bandusian spring. The caretaker has come down from the little shack where, with fire, wine, and transistor radio he passes his days waiting for the occasional visitor to come and sign the register left open on the low wall which marks the outline of the villa. He is a plain, husky, florid man who has his own pride of place. One day, sitting out of sight against the wall and reading his newspaper, he heard two visitors come up the rocky path, stop at the low wall to glance at the clearing, say to each other, "It's only a tomb," and leave without visiting the grounds.

So fast and furious was the reaction of the caretaker that he quickly jotted down on the margin of his newspaper an indignant verse entitled *Reazione del custode* (The Caretaker's Response) wherein he noted that in other days, filled with frescoes and fountains and the step of the great poet, the villa was quite other than a tomb, and even now, old and fallen, it is not a tomb because the memory of Horace lives on in the thoughts of every civil person who comes to the site.

He is quite right. Go there on a spring day when the grass floor of the villa is carpeted with bluebells and daisies and a delicious breeze is blowing across the Licenza valley; walk through the ground plan into outlines of rooms that are indelibly associated with Horace, and walk down the avenues which were once-porticoed approaches to the main entrance and hold between them the huge clumps of fragrant rosemary that were in the poet's garden, and view the depression where his grand pool once glimmered; recall the verses of his supreme contentment, his happy phrases, and retrace his path up to the spring—*O fons Bandusiae, splendidior vitro* . . . which is now corniced in stone bearing Orsini arms in a baroque flourish. From where we are we can look down in the distance to a pink house with smoke curling from a chimney and deck chairs on a terrace: it belongs to an English couple newly arrived in the valley. The English have a knack for classical sites; but then they always were the champion quoters of Horace, except for Lord Byron who wrote him off with, "Then farewell Horace, whom I hated so."

The caretaker of the Sabine farm has also written a poem about the spring which he shows us. He is a simple man and there are some mistakes: for *eco* (echo) he has mistakenly written ego so that he speaks of the falling spring giving Horace a "profound ego" rather than an echo. Or perhaps this is extreme subtlety, a Freudian-Joycean play on words and meanings. The caretaker says he was televised once—a team came out from Rome to give him and his poetry a spot on the *Chronicle of Italy* program which precedes the nightly news; but it was July and who, he asks, sadly, is indoors at 8 P.M. in July to watch television? *Sunt lacrimae rerum*. . . . We all have our misfortunes.

Maecenas gave Horace his farm when the poet was thirty-two; for the next twenty-five years, until he died in 8 B.C. at the age of fifty-seven, Horace lived a country life composing his odes, overseeing his farm, going less and less to Rome. Horace called his farm modest, but it was a twelve-room villa on extensive grounds to which he added a grander suite of baths and better plumbing than had been there originally. There were two courtyards with sculptured fountains (fragments of which can be seen in the museum at Licenza where all extant artifacts are kept), a summer dining room and a winter one, mosaic pavements and frescoed walls.

Horace loved it:

This was one of the things I used to pray for
a parcel of land, not over-large, with a garden
and near the house a spring that would always be flowing
and a little woodland besides
Bigger and better is this that the Gods
have done for me. All is well. *Bene est.*

From what was the Digentia valley, Horace profers excuses to Maecenas for preferring country life to the city ("Small things go well with small people"), invites Vergil to come, but bring his own wine ("Come with your merchandise / for I mean not to give free wine / as if a wealthy house were mine"), extols old-time virtue in a preachy ode addressed to the Romans, compares himself as poet first to the humble bumblebee, then to a monument more durable than brass, tells the tale of the town mouse and the country mouse drawing the appropriate moral, expounds the golden mean, seems content in an ode to Venus to have hung up his girl-charming lute and turned philosophical, and sets out precepts for beginning writers in which he enjoins them to avoid the *pannus purpureus* (purple patch) in writing. He is the soul of equanimity and reason—imperturbable, Epicurean in his love of life, Stoic in his gallant refusal to despair before the inevitable nothingness.

In a real sense Horace asks more of himself than a believer could. No matter how bad things go in this life, the believer is buoyed by the thought of future happiness and fulfillment. Horace's message is tougher, existentialist almost: live for the day for this is all we have, but nonetheless, all things in moderation and don't despair; or, in Dryden's version:

> Happy the man, and happy he alone,
> He who can call today his own;
> He who, secure within, can say
> Tomorrow, do thy worst for I have liv'd today.

Horace endures, wise and civilized and speaking to all ages. But especially, perhaps, to our own. Certainly Horace's retiring to his country place to walk in the porticoed alleys alongside his garden, meditate at the Bandusian spring, and think things out in his poetry is not at all a bad recipe for today's more and more frantic society. But with the work week and the Protestant Work

Ethic all receding, people today are clearly called upon to devote themselves to other than digging and delving. Not for naught the interest in Yoga and meditation and other attractions of the East through which we are called upon to transcend material ties and become whole. Herman Kahn, a different kind of guru, who founded the Hudson Institute think tank to think out worst-case scenarios during the cold-war years, cautiously predicted from the year 2000-on an age of ascendant hippyism.

Gregory Corso, a poet less suave than Horace, put it this way: "It won't be long before everyone will sit in bed and eat big fat pies. They got machines now to do the work. People got to start thinking. That's what's going to save us. Everyone staying in bed eating big fat pies and thinking."

Neither Kahn nor Corso could be taken for the prophetic Sibyl of the Tibur, but trends do point to more free time, more time to think; more time to live as Horace did. In Rome, do as the Romans do. I took Horace to heart. I liked his messages about avoiding purple patches in writing and keeping a golden mean in life. *Carpe diem* he famously said; value independence, maintain a civilized balance of wisdom, humor, and tact, live the day simply and well.

Neruda vs. Sartre at the Sea

They tell of certain years in the Italian literary-prize business as the French would speak of a good or bad vintage year: the giddy splendors of 1970 prize-feting and fighting, the multiple crises of '68 culminating in the sad death of Nobel poet Salvatore Quasimodo while presiding at some minor poetry prize event at Amalfi and the year Moravia, out of pique or paradox, went on to found his own prize, giving the first award to his ex-wife in lieu (it's said) of support payments.

Italian literati have more prizes for each other than there are grapes in all of the Loire. And enough gossip about them during the lulls to provide endless *storielle*—always dearer to competing writers than tales of switches among lovers or spouses or sexes.

There was a week during the summer of 1967, just following the brief Israel-Arab War, when Viareggio was, for a moment, raised from provincial to almost global splendor. It would make a great Fellini movie. It was the year of Big Names at the seaside.

The stretch of Tuscany bordering on the Tyrrhenian Sea would be the setting, and, specifically, the resort of Viareggio, a once-uninhabited sand beach backed by thick strands of umbrella pines not far from where Percy Shelley's drowned body was washed up. Viareggio is now a flat, ugly Vacationville where an ugly bronze head of the poet has been stuck on a shaft opposite the post-office to remember him. The famous pines are brown, dry sticks dying—dead—of fumes and the depredations of those hordes who now throng the sea and churn it from blue to brown; the beach is paved over, squalid with shops, jammed with miles and miles of beach apparatus and bodies. The sea is a sewer of floating fruit skins, plastic bags, eggshells, urine. It has all the melancholy of Fellini's resort town in his film *I Vitelloni.*

Now imagine a turn-of-the-century hotel once called Grand, now called Royal, but actually neither. It has been the scene each summer for over fifty years (excluding only two occupation years of World War II) of the literary prize which is Italy's oldest, best, richest, most prestigious, most leftist, out of a national total of 338 such awards. Here will gather the characters who make up the prize contingent. Outside the hotel a kind of gray smoke-screen (which everyone refers to as this *foschia terribile*) lies over each day almost as if such density of literati at Viareggio had raised its own pall of smog, as if these lethal fumes were trying to render the frenetic semblance of local life as dead and brown as the pine-woods.

Inside, talk, the literary form of action, takes place in the hotel lobby in overstuffed armchairs placed around tables loaded with brochures—"The Versilian Riviera offers you sunshine, gentle warm seas, golden sands, the shade of delightful pine trees. . . . Don't forget to go, because you won't forget you came." Talk continues on the dining terrace under a charming green arbor (perhaps plastic) that, withal, still can't dispel the sense of dread melancholy which the ineluctable backdrop of dead pines bestows. Waiters, headwaiters, a sommelier, prosciutto with figs and eggs in aspic are all there. Despite the haughty stance of the dining room staff, the complicated ceremony of serving runs down constantly with a surfeit of waiters producing overcooked pasta, withered salad, the wrong orders or no orders at all.

The bulk of the guests at the Grand-Royal are the twenty-two jurists of the Viareggio Literary prize who are there with their families (all expenses paid) to distribute twenty-eight-million lire in prizes to the various writers, poets, scholars, who will be off-scene until Award Night.

Principal among the assembled characters is Leonida Répaci (already an old Fellini hand, he played himself, the gabby intellectual, in *La Dolce Vita*), President-Founder of the Viareggio Prize and still indefatigable after scores of summers of it and equally as many novels, but slightly more hallucinatory each succeeding year. Répaci has white hair, wild blue eyes, and is a combination of Charles Ruggles as the White Rabbit in *Alice in Wonderland*, and Mr. Dick in *David Copperfield*. He is constantly running around in shorts and sandals, clapping his hands to round up dawdling jurists, herding them to conferences, haranguing them to be on time. He is followed by a prim duenna-wife who wears dark glasses and hair rollers under a scarf, and a large-bosomed, jovial secretary.

Among the distinguished cast there'll be Goffredo Parise who had won a Viareggio prize for his book *Il Padrone* (The Boss) and has now been raised from the contention to jurist. He is just back from Vietnam and likes to assume a boy-ruffian pose. He is credited with much expertise in the matter of vote-swapping, promissory actions, plotting, etc. They say he won the five-million-lire Viareggio prize the year before by having his claque withdraw their support from the one-million-lire Strega Prize to risk everything on the larger haul. His passing onto the jury, signals, perhaps, that his years of enfant terrible are at an end—he's approaching forty. He now aspires to a certain casual, sporty elegance and is concerned about his paunch. He asks sartorial advice of Countess Piovene who points out that his trousers trail unfashionably over his sandals. During the whole convocation he will maintain a mysterious Chinese air (he's also back from China) and indulge in much whispering and tête-à-têting to advance his protégés. He's successful at everything, including dancing the

Shake with Signora Buzzati, wife of fellow jurist and famous writer Dino Buzzati.

Giuseppe Ungaretti, old and beloved poet, who is announced on the roster of names as a jurist, will, however, be conspicuous by his absence as he's gone off to London to read poetry with Allen Ginsburg, Pablo Neruda, Ted Hughes.

Guido and Mimi Piovene are there. He, the jurist, is pale and quiet. He goes to the beach under a large sombrero and is subject to a nervous tic of lip-twisting. A Veneto aristocrat with leftist sympathies, he is known as the Red Count and lives, he has declared, only to write. His wife Mimi is an affable, elegant blonde with a static hairdo and a luxury wardrobe of clothes which she constantly changes. She is known as The Firmament for the great sparkle of her jewels, or as The Madonna di Loreto for the quantity of them. She drives a blue Skylark and speaks French on the beach.

Maria Luisa Astaldi is a jurist, editor, scholar, TV consultant, Socialist, and a formidable literary lady who admires Mrs. Gaskell and detests American air-conditioning to the point of foregoing some important cultural confab in New York because of it. She is always attired in expensive pants outfits with kooky stockings showing above glittering ball slippers. She will refuse to go to the reception organized by Répaci's secretary and offered by a rich Milanese manufacturer who vacations nearby because ladies don't attend the affairs of garment-makers. She smiles a Cheshire Cat smile and has a chauffeur who drives her around the countryside for lunch or museum viewing. Her husband can't bear Viareggio; he's cruising off Elba in their yacht waiting for her. Despite her admiration for the Anglo-American world, she needles TV personality Ruggiero Orlando about his not using a fish knife, attributing this to his too-long residence in the United States. Someone replies that the Duke of Bedford also dismisses the fish knife as a contemptible upstart used only in bourgeois (and socialist?)

households since it was not introduced until Queen Victoria's reign and anyone who is anyone will have table silver that is Georgian or earlier. Of such preciousness is the table talk at Viareggio composed.

Giorgio Caproni, a gaunt, graying poet and jurist with an old-fashioned crew cut, says be won't go to the USA because all the food there is canned. This reinforces his old-fashioned air and is amusing to hear at a pretentious Italian hotel where canned peas, canned fruit cup, and frozen fish are served. It marks him as a true poet. The other Italian intellectuals will have more austere reasons for hating America—Vietnam, affluence, influence, conveniences, insipience, resilience, air-conditioning, ice cubes, etc. Caproni, like many other poets living on modest teachers' salaries, supplements it by vacationing on the literary prize circuit: besides expenses, jurists receive honorariums.

Milena Milani, an ex-bella, is a dark, square-faced author whose sunburn gives her a Native American look. She is a perpetual attendant at these literary occasions along with Maria Luisa Spaziani, called L'Armoire, a great big figure of a poetess who also looms ever-present at literary do's. Both women have already had their haul of prizes and Milena now has the added distinction of a novel being banned.

Libero Bigiaretti, another writer and head of the Italian Writers' Union, is an ex-Viareggio jurist and a mere onlooker this year. He assumes an anti-literary pose as he does at every book launching, publisher's cocktail party, prize ceremony, book promotion deal, etc., at which he always shows up. He effects to look off into distances and from time to time mutters, "Is it possible these people can't see the irony of all this?"

Other jurists are scholars and university professors. They are serious, erudite, dignified men who walk about with multilingual newspapers and books, and try to be in bed by 11:30. They are Communist or tending that way, or have been that way and are tending out. There is a fine scene where they're pulled by leggy, bikini-clad black Brazilian chorus-girls onto the dance-floor at a nightclub where Répaci's secretary has organized an evening for them with free champagne (but an inferior Italian brand, they will complain later).

The wives of the austere professors will outdo themselves in an outdated show of conspicuous consumption. One is said to have spent half a million lire on her Viareggio outfits; another has a navy blue chauffeur-driven limousine; another goes off daily to buy fabulous antiques in Lucca. In looks and tastes and habits they are indistinguishable from the wives of American capitalists except that they—the Commies—live better. The paradox doesn't present itself and no one is rude enough to mention it, except in the whisperings of a few Catholic malcontents who would like to go all the way left and live in such style but don't dare.

Fellini's script should bring out the factions, counter-factions, and factious factions at this literary bazaar. The effects of the six-day Israel-Arab conflict are still in the air and have a bearing on the confabulations. The hard-core Communists stand with Nasser and the Arabs, while those who are Communist and Jewish are caught on the horns of the dilemma. The ex-fascists are now the moralizing section of the jury; the Catholics will be constantly looking for a chance at "dialogue;" and the old-time anticlericals will gleefully relate that Pope Paul VI is actually Eichmann (witness, they say, that same featureless, functionary face and drab manner), and that the real Paul VI was kidnapped and hung in Eichmann's place. This explains the Vatican's pro-Arab line.

Walk-on parts will abound in this film: recognizable aspiring women intellectuals, the hosts and hostesses of the literati, and just plain hangers-on in the service of authors in the running at Viareggio who will keep their authors informed of which way the wind blows by listening in to lobby talk. This is essential so that authors who know they can't make it can send a wire to the jury and "withdraw" their books at the last minute, thus saving face. This will be used by a noted woman writer whose first ploy, having her husband take a leave of absence from the Viareggio jury for this summer so that her book could be in the lists, was construed by the jurists as having all the delicacy of a Mafia threat.

There will be appearances every now and then by husky, tattooed, blue-eyed and bronzed Americans in soiled tee shirts and denims who pass through the lobby on their way to the bar looking curiously at the literary types; the Americans are hale, hearty, loud, and are at Viareggio for an international speedboat race to Corsica and back. They'll stay totally ignorant of the literary prize business and assume that the hotel is filled with people to see the start-off of their race.

There are hotel lobby type people, too, including two old Dukes of the House of Savoy, cousins of the late King Vittorio Emmanuele II, who turn up every summer without fail at the Grand-Royal and assist impassively with their Buster Keaton faces at the Award Night ceremony. Daily they pass through the lobby on their way to the beach across the street in deep red and deep blue terry cloth bathrobes from which their spindly legs make startling white exclamation points.

During the Award Night scene we'll see the en masse arrival of a Queens College professor, his wife and daughters, and the group of seventeen students they've brought abroad for a summer of Italian culture and life at Viareggio. The professor has wangled a whole block of seats for Award Night from Répaci by deeply touching the old organizer at the thought that for these Americans his Viareggio Prize will be the chief cultural event of their summer—perhaps of their lives.

From time to time we will see the enormous table on the dining terrace which accommodates the twenty-two jurists and several secretaries. There will be lively discussions for each category of award with groups pushing their candidates against those of other groups, maneuverings, concessions, pledges, conclusions; but the liveliest discussion will be for the International Prize which is the year's innovation (in the hope of keeping dwindling attention focused on the Viareggio Prize which, though first, best, wisest, etc., is yearly losing ground to upstart imitative prizes). With the grand gesture of five million lire to an International star who "has spent his very life for culture, understanding amongst peoples, and peace," Répaci aims to keep Viareggio in the forefront and add new luster to a flagging institution.

A lot of big names are tossed around the big table: Jean-Paul Sartre, Pablo Neruda, Peter Weiss, Lewis Mumford, Bemard Russell, Robert Lowell. One jurist proposes Rafael Alberti, the Spanish anti-Franco poet who has been living in exile in Italy the past thirty years—an excellent poet, an honest man, and someone who could use the money. The proposal will fall effortlessly and it is clear that the battle will be between Sartre and Neruda. The film dialogue must follow certain lines: the hard-core Communists, the practical-minded, and the disoriented will back Neruda; mixed-sentimentalists, idealists, and the remaining disoriented will back Sartre.

There's a heated skirmish as to whether Sartre, who declined a Nobel, will bother with Viareggio. Someone will say that Sartre only refused the Nobel because it wasn't given to him the year he wanted it. Hoots of derision and catcalls will follow this. Some will say that Sartre is the only name of enough stature to dignify the prize and establish it securely for the future. The practical will rejoin that the prize—and they, the jurists—will be the laughing stock of the literary world if, as seems certain, Sartre doesn't show up.

An organized woman jurist points out that Neruda has been making the international scene lately and is a professional by now at going around to poetry readings and collecting prizes; he'll turn up at Viareggio for sure. In fact, someone notes, Neruda is already in London; another says that he can easily be here by Saturday—look how easy it is for Jackie Onassis to get a plane and come down to Marli for dinner, just a few miles away.

There will be shouting, vituperations, then Répaci will hammer for silence and call for a vote between Sartre and Neruda. The decision for Neruda will bring the vigorous architect Bruno Zevi, leader of the Sartrian faction, to his feet to call out forthrightly, "I consider any vote against Sartre as a vote against Israel!"

Confusion and babel; jurists rise to their feet and protest. Shouting, indignation, a free-for-all. An excellent movie scene. It is the high point of the film, almost as good as last year's scene when Moravia engaged Répaci in fisticuffs.

In conclusion the Sartrians will append a paragraph to the International Award proclamation in which they list themselves by name as having voted for Sartre. The Catholics will mutter that these things are always leftist and the big money always goes to the Communists. But all passions will be spent that evening at the midnight beach supper organized by Répaci's indefatigable secretary, who got a local restaurateur to put on the supper at the beach with such specialties as *frutta del mare*, cabbage and bean soup, codfish with cornmeal, and lollipops for desert. Countess Piovene will dress grandly for the event and rescue a rather miserable affair by pronouncing the dishes "regional" and thus endowing them with an aura of folklore. In any case, a free festa is a great pacifier.

Pablo Neruda, a big stentorian-voiced man, does arrive the following evening and reads his poems in a ringing, revivalist voice before collecting his check and departing. No word from Sartre. Festivities dissolve after a Boost-Viareggio group puts on a playlet by a local hippie about the coming revolution which the audience will watch ungraciously, making unkind remarks, yawning, talking, moving about. Only the royal dukes, impassive and correct as always, will watch the performing beatniks with good manners and applause. All this to the background din of the American boat-men in the bar who still haven't figured out what's been going on.

The last scene will be a mêlée as jurists and prize winners ac-cost the buffet table under the shepherding of Répaci and his wife, now rollerless and couched in a many-colored, batwing-sleeved organza fantasy. The rest of the audience drifts out into the noisy smoggy Viareggio night.

But that's not the real end. That will come the following sum-mer with the arrival of that year's prize-designate Italo Calvino's telegram: "Believing the era of literary prizes definitely over and done with, I wish to decline the Viareggio award. I cannot endorse with my acceptance an institution now empty of all significance."

The old order is breaking up all over. In the summer of '67, women's lib is looming over the horizon; the sit-ins of winter '67–'68 when the students of Rome University chanted "*Mao, si, Moravia no!*" are imminent; soon the moon itself will be no longer inviolate and some American called Mario Puzo will break records in Italy with a book called *The Godfather* to the indignation of real Italian writers.

Prizes won't ever again be as factious, fashionable, or funny. And there will be regrets. As Bigiaretti observed: "These prize ceremonies take the place of Renaissance courts with their pa-trons and protegés and carriers of favor and poets in search of laurel." And the pleasantry at Viareggio in the summer of '67 was that the poets of today are not so interested in laurel as in gather-ing together enough other green stuff in lire-bills for the rest of their days.

But after many a summer dies even that swan.

Souvenirs of Venice

Whiffs of death: the reading group I lead at the library is discussing *Death in Venice*. My thoughts wander as the dozen or so readers extract the story's symbols—the cemetery and the ominous sense of fatigue and storm enveloping Aschenbach on the opening page; the coffin-like gondola, the gondolier as Charon crossing the Styx; the smell of plague, the flight of the vacationers, the sickliness of Tadzio. They talk, they assume I listen. I do not. I am thinking not of Death, but of Antonio (who was my husband), in Venice.

I see him in a photo as I never knew him in life; as Canaletto painted, with almost imperceptible sleight of hand. Canaletto's Venice painted in such a cunning way, with such typically Venetian mirroring artifice, to make it seem as if I am looking at verisimilitude when I survey his light-drenched canvases. I could swear that Piazza San Marco, looking toward the Clock Tower, is exactly that way until the explanatory legend next to the painting gives it away—what appears completely real is just mostly real. Canaletto depicts the piazzetta with the lion of St. Mark atop its column, a corner of the Marciana library, a bridge, and the Church of Santa Maria della Salute all at once—an elegant impossibility, a stunning picture. It makes no difference. I know where I am. It *is* Venice.

And this young man of twenty or so, summering on the Lido with his Venetian cousins, though not the one I knew, *is* Antonio: he is lounging lengthwise in a beached *sandalo*, his head indolently supported in the palm of one hand as his arm rests on the seat. He is a lithe, bronzed Adonis, slim and muscular, with pointy ears and a sly-fox smile of provocation beamed over a separating ocean to signal me a beckoning Italy. I am a child of two or three in the unpromising landscape of central New York, far from any sea. How would I know of him from so far away? Because I dreamt him.

An earlier scene from his family's album: it is the morning of July 14, 1902. Antonio has not been born; I have not been born, yet something happens in Venice in the predawn of that summer day that colors our sense of the place and sticks like a family event in both our minds—but now only in mine, since Antonio is many years dead.

So on that day of 1902, as occurred every morning of her married life, angular, long-faced Arcangela Barolini who resembles lean Doge Loredan of the Bellini portrait and who will be Antonio's grandmother in years to come, throws open the *persiane* that shutter the windows of her Venice home to greet the scene and look out upon the early day to see what is in store. She is a wife and mother, an early riser, an industrious woman who knows how to keep accounts, run a household, prepare a *strudel di gris*, write amusing letters to her ship captain husband away at sea, and take life in the Venetian manner—poking fun at it because it is so serious.

Arcangela lives with her ancient parents, her husband (when he's there), and her only child (the handsome, dark, wavy-haired son who will go to sea as a naval officer and then marry and become Antonio's father). They live on the top floor of an old Venetian palazzo within window-sight of the campanile of Piazza San Marco. The campanile, tall and elegant like her son, is the familiar beginning of Arcangela's mornings. All through the day she hears chimes of varying register, by which she can tell the time, from the brick bell tower.

This day, the shutters flung back, she leans out, looks, shakes her head as if to clear her brain of any lingering sleep-state, strains her eyes to look again, and then gasps in disbelief. *Mah! Non zé più!* she calls out excitedly, alarming the household who run to her side and look out with her at the emptiness. In fact, there is no more campanile; during the night the old brick tower had silently shuddered, hung breathless in the air an instant, then collapsed of its great age, like an elegantly fainting Victorian dame, into a tremendous heap of bricks on the square. For nine hundred years it has always been there, and now it isn't. (Ten years later, in 1912 when the tower is once again in place and the square looks the same as it ever did, Thomas Mann will be in Venice composing in an incandescent dazzle his story of Aschenbach and the beautiful Tadzio.)

July 14th, which in some parts is celebrated as Bastille Day, is known in Venice as the day the tower fell. It is the favorite story of Antonio's childhood. Two faint sepia-tinted photographs in the family album show an incredible sight: a mountain of rubble in the piazza dwarfs the men who stand with brooms and shovels at its edges; behind the mass of fallen brick, imperturbable, exquisite, serene as La Serenissima herself, and untouched, are the basilica of St. Mark's and the Doge's palace. And there, also unscathed, is an angle of the Marciana against which the bricks are heaped, and the long colonnades of the Procuratorie Vecchie and the Procuratorie Nuove, so familiar from Canaletto. These are the buildings, called the "Old" and "New" government houses because they once served as residences for the solicitor general overseeing the buildings of St. Mark's, which effectively frame the square, and are known by sight to all the world with their wealth of shops and elegant old Caffè Florian within the arched porticos. The older, sixteenth-century structure is the one adjoining the

Clock Tower where the blackamoors come out to sound the hours, and is the only privately owned residence on the piazza. It is at this time occupied by Signora Levi.

In her forty-room apartment, the widow Levi rises much later than Arcangela; and, with a great deal more calm, will gaze out silently and wonderingly from one of the sixteen long, graceful windows which overlook the piazza at the hillock of crumbled bricks below. She was told of the event by the maid who opened the blinds of the rococo bedroom and served the first tiny cup of black coffee with which the signora is daily awakened.

Signora Levi is a dignified, handsome woman of strict custom. Well-read, well-bred, she is reserved and rather too lacking in spirit to be considered a beauty; she leads a quiet, almost reclusive life often stretched out on her dormeuse reading Carolina Invernizio novels. Where Arcangela bustles, Signora Levi is languid. The former is dark, the latter fair. Widowed at age twenty-seven, Signora Levi never remarried but stayed on in the fabulous apartment in the Old Government House with her two young sons and with a staff of servants to see to her wants and needs. The cook only cooks; for the shopping and preparing of food there are kitchen assistants. Signora Levi's personal maid takes care of her person and nothing else; her personal gondolier awaits her bidding. In the household there are other servants, and for the whole, an administrator who comes daily to his office in that building which is now a national monument.

On the morning of July 14, 1902, Signora Levi sits at a dressing table bright with chinoiserie as her maid slips a delicately embroidered matinée of cool lawn over her shoulders and begins to brush out the signora's long locks, once a fulvous amber and now dulled with silver. Her chamber, closed by two-meter-high doors of pistachio-green lacquer highlighted with gilded scrollwork and divided into four panels of allegorical figures, all embellished with decorative garlands or ribbons and bows, is a sight to behold; the ceiling is high and light; sun filters through the blinds onto a plant stand fashioned from a sculpted cherub caught within the branches of a flowering laurel and holding aloft a shell-like basin in which reposes a vivid cyclamen.

The room is filled with charming eighteenth-century lacquered pieces, brought, it's possible, from Portuguese Goa and its China trade in the very sailing ships of Antonio's sea-captain forebears, perhaps in the vessel *San Spiridione* which will give title to Antonio's first book of poetry. The look of the room is light and graceful; its ornamentation and voluptuousness wash against Signora Levi at her every glance and move without ever engulfing, or even so much as bathing her with its lambent glow. She is distantly aware of, but not submerged by, the beauty. She is not Aschenbach.

Everything in casa Levi is of museum quality: the silk headboard with its gilt volutes, the graceful, damask-upholstered bench at the foot of the bed, the tilt-top table with a magnificent central landscape surrounded by eight medallions of eighteenth-century ladies and cavaliers in various poses, the rattan dormeuse in the corner next to the bombé chest, the chiffonier, and the delicate chair with the floral sprays and openwork back like a figure eight on which the signora sits facing her toilette mirror. The prettily framed floral mirror is part of the opened lid of the *arte povera* box in which Signora Levi keeps her everyday jewels and trinkets. (It is called a "poor art" box because the exterior is covered with découpage figures and vases to simulate painting and only the interior is actually painted in the Chinese manner. Many years after Signora Levi's demise, and after the Second World War has scattered her descendants to America and elsewhere and her furnishings to flea markets, that arte povera box will turn up in Perugia where Antonio will find it and make a gift of it to me; and now, somewhat flaked by time and travel, some of its figures dimmed, it sits atop an antique chest in the bedroom of my West-chester apartment.)

In 1902 Signora Levi's sons are grown and no longer at home to see the sight of the fallen campanile. One is a pediatrician in Trieste, the other a professor at the University of Turin; both are distinguished, and between them they have eleven children to send on vacations to the grandmother in Venice. One of these children, a daughter of the Trieste pediatrician, was Federica who is now in my library reading group listening intently to the discussion of *Death in Venice*. Federica never speaks at these meetings. Federica is an enigma.

And just as she visited her grandmother in Venice, so, too, did Antonio from his home in Vicenza in the old Venetian terra firma. In snapshots I see him, age three, in his *nonna* Arcangela's court-yard. He is dressed in what I instantly recognize as a version of my once-loathed Convent School uniform, a boxy long-sleeved navy blue tunic with pleated front and below-waist belt. It looks better on the child Antonio than on me the recalcitrant adolescent, both because he had a better attitude toward wearing it and be-cause his is topped with a sumptuous lace mantle that could have adorned a cardinal. Again, age eight or nine he is there beside the well in the Venetian courtyard, this time with his little sister Mariarcangela. Antonio is dressed in a white sailor suit that comes to his knees, t-strap sandals and prettily worked socks; he has wonderful thick, dark wavy hair and an open smile and his hand is protectively on his sister. He has given his wonderful hair to our three girls, and these pictures are a miracle to me as I see in those beguiling, old-fashioned children in faraway Venice the looks and features of my American daughters.

In his boyhood, on long summer days, Antonio would wander through the rios and calles of Venice. He was to find, in the Palla-dian church of San Francesco della Vigna in an out-of-the way campo, a votive offering from one of his sea captain ancestors who had been saved from a storm at sea by the sudden, miraculous apparition on deck of the Blessed Mother. Another ancestor, Sebastiano Barolini, not so fortunate, was swept overboard the night his wife gave birth to their child, Emerita Anna, whose portrait hangs on my apartment wall.

Federica, granddaughter of Signora Levi, has faithfully attended the book group from its inception without ever taking part in a discussion. She is widowed and retired from work—a silent, grayhaired woman hunched over an open book at the far end of the table, eyes down. She wears thick wool sweaters in muted shades. I strain to picture her, a dark-haired young woman, in Signora Levi's japanned drawing room, in the flickering mercurial light of Venice.

It was her Italian name on the reading group's sign-up sheet that made me seek out Federica and speak to her in Italian. I was nostalgic for Italy where I lived a good part of my marriage. She waved her hand dismissively: "Oh! it's so long since I lived there—another life!"

"But you must have kept things—photos, souvenirs."

"When I should have kept things, I didn't," Federica said, shaking her head, "and now it's too late. Everything's gone."

Getting Federica to reminisce is like trying to pry fossilized remains from an unyielding matrix. She is bemused at my fascination with the past, my return to it over and over; for her it is at best irrelevant, at worst a burden.

Federica laughs away my questions: "Who wants to think of those days? Everyone was so strict then! I could never do what I wanted. At my grandmother's in Venice we weren't even permitted to say *Addio* because it names God. Why should I remember?"

I, instead, am an incurable collector of mementos. Packed and repacked and carried to all my homes in a green velvet box with brass corners, are heaps of photos of my family and of Antonio's. His are more interesting—because they're snapped in Venice, on the Lido, or at country homes in the Veneto—and because I know the people from his stories. There is *zia* Marietta Faccioli before whose name appear the letters N.D. for *nobil donna*, who, during the nineteenth-century Austrian occupation of Venice indignantly approached an Imperial Officer and told him to lift his sword from the ground where it dragged since it wasn't worthy of touching Italian soil. There is lovely, delicate *zia* Giulia, for whom my Susanna Giulia is named and whose look (the Albarello side) Susi has. Tiny and spry, *zia* Giulia lived into her eighties hiking intrepidly with her husband through the Dolomites and publishing a monthly bulletin called the *Crusade Against Blasphemy*. When, as a young bride I was momentarily disoriented and homesick in Vicenza, it was she who tossed her wide-brimmed straw hat out the window of our top floor apartment and let it go sailing off toward the Public Gardens to cheer me up. There is Caterina Crivellari, Antonio's maternal grandmother, called Catin in the family, whose boarding school notebook of the 1860s, bound in parchment, is kept with the albums. She was a dashing woman with a mound of hair which she dressed in fantastic shapes, and she looks as if she might have given *nonno* Gregorio a bit of a time. Pictured in his sailor suit when he was an apprentice machinist on a naval ship, is Antonio's tall, dark father from whom our first child gets her stature. Then there are all the postcard portraits of kith and kin which were regularly sent back and forth to each other to show a new hat, a new child, a view from a trip. I have things from Venice—a Ciardi painting, a *maschera* puppet, furnishings, maps and books, the replicas of Antonio's ancestors' sailing ships, a huge log charting all the Mediterranean ports and used in the coastal trade known as *cabotaggio*.

Federica has nothing of all that. She shrugs at the past. What is this basic, urgent, essential call to Italy in my life that left such an imprint on me? Was it my premonition of Antonio? And am I still connected to that second homeland because I left Antonio behind in a grave in Vicenza, while Federica, though fleeing the Jewish persecution of World War II, came to the States with a husband and a family still intact? Federica came from Italy to leave the old and start a new life; I left behind in Italy what was my new life.

Still, I often wonder about the unvoiced loss she must feel.

I know what mine is. Does Federica's weigh in greater on the scale of losses? I had come to Italy as another homeland. Federica and her family were sent out from it by the coming terror. Her way of life was long gone. "My dowry!" she once exclaimed ironically of her trousseau bed linen. "And can you imagine, a whole line of maids' uniforms with hand-embroidered organdy aprons and head caps? And dozens of nightgowns!—silk with Brussels lace. I still have a few—my daughters won't touch them. Who's going to bother to hand-wash and press them? they say. Can you imagine such things these days?"

Yes, I can imagine. Federica's dowry was a more sumptuous version of my own immigrant grandmother's Calabrian spreads of thick homespun cotton, towels with long fringes of flax that were once reserved for the doctor who, in those days, made house calls and then washed his hands, and ample nightgowns made deliberately wide to accommodate the expected pregnancies. Those fringed towels, the spreads, the huge nightgowns are in the fifteenth-century chest that was the first piece Antonio and I bought after our marriage. But as Federica says, who of our daughters now wants them?

I met Federica's family when they invited me to a party in her honor at her retirement as a social worker. It was held in the dark, windowless room of a Ramada Inn where an overwhelmingly plentiful brunch was served from huge metal warmers. The place was filled with people I did not know. Federica wore a black dress and a string of pearls and had on her shoulder an orchid corsage. Smiling and happy, she was surrounded by friends, coworkers, her two daughters and two sons, their spouses, and all the grandchildren. I was as silent at the party as Federica is at the book group. I wondered if any room would be filled with family and friends when I reached seventy. If it happens, one of those present will be Federica, and the room will be flooded with light from windows open to a view; inside there will be jars of blue iris and only champagne and raspberry meringue will be served.

Things were unraveling for me on many fronts when I ran into Federica at the supermarket: "I'm going to move—I'm alone now. The house is too big. Is anything available here where you live?"

She invited me to her condo townhouse, a bargain, she said, because there were no frills. The place was heated electrically and Federica kept the heat down and piled on sweaters. It was very cold. Her living room was furnished in the squarish, heavy-legged thirties style which gave a foreign-movie look to everything. The rooms were smallish, the people in the other units looked unappealing. I was a snob. I didn't take the empty unit two doors down from Federica. And I remember thinking, how could she, with her past life, end up here?

It was bleak February when I moved elsewhere. I was exhausted, demoralized. Federica had me come for a bite to eat the evening of my move. "But I haven't gone out to shop," she warned.

In her kitchen where the table was set with Pennsylvania Dutch dishes on plastic mats of the Grand Canyon, I watched her fuss at a stove to which she continually addressed insults. "Tell me about Trieste," I said, sipping the glass of V-8 juice that was at my place. Like an out-of-place refugee, a silver *oliera* (the compartmentalized cruet stand for oil and vinegar, salt and pepper which I always remember on the table of Antonio's Vicenza home) stood in the center of the table. I knew that Federica's girlhood in Trieste had coincided with the period that James Joyce lived there.

"You're interested in the literary circles—Svevo and Joyce and all that—but I paid no attention to any of those people. I was a child . . . I found them dull. Like Stanislaus Joyce who taught my father English—we all laughed at him, he was so gauche. My father himself occasionally helped Joyce out. But who cared in those days? How could I know he'd be famous?"

The bite to eat turned out to be a many-coursed dinner including fish done with a light vinagrette and onion sauce that had aromatic overtones of the Veneto and brought to mind the time I had spent in the region early in my marriage. With my move I had gone over and packed all the family things—the portrait of Antonio's great-aunt Emerita Anna, the correspondence of Antonio with his father, a naval officer hospitalized in La Spezia, the barometer and sextant from the sailing ships of the Barolinis of Venice who had been of such probity and skill that they had been granted the privilege of transporting the Doge's gold *zecchini* in their sailing ships. How much stuff, how many talismans I had brought over from their world to mine!

"What does it feel like to lose the past, Federica?"

Was I asking Federica what it felt like to be transplanted, or still asking myself? Was I disapproving of Federica's non-attachment to the past, her lack of memory—of photos, even—or skeptical of mine? Do we disapprove in others what we most fear in ourselves?

"Maybe it took just such an upheaval in order to be able to change," Federica answered in an even tone.

Now at the library where the discussion of *Death in Venice* swirls around me, I wonder about all that.

Wise Federica, I think, seeing her wrapped in silence and gray. She hasn't lost anything. Where she lands, she is. She transforms her reality; she has what she wants: her freedom, her reading, her family nearby, her sense of herself without the old photos, without the maids in organdy aprons, and without the wondrous rooms of a grandmother in Venice.

Being at Bellagio

In a late spring of some years ago I was racked with doubts: a completed novel, still unpublished, was in a drawer awaiting not only a publisher but even an agent who would represent it and send it out to some welcoming editor. And I was planning another book about six American women writers and how Italy had played into their lives. Their stories connected with my own discovery of Italy where I had begun to write, had married an Italian writer, and had lived for some years. But entwined with the pleasure I took in planning a new book was the risk that it, too, could end up in a drawer. For what was the point of writing without being realized in print and brought to readers? Was I indulging in false hopes, a dotty dame, now living and working alone, finding no outlet for my work?

And then one Friday returning home from my library job and playing back my telephone messages, I heard the director of the Rockefeller Foundation's Bellagio Center asking if I were still able to accept a residency at their Center on Lake Como. I had previously applied without success. Now I was their first choice of three alternates to replace a professor who had had a heart attack and dropped dead on his lawn the day before he was to arrive in Italy. Would I be ready to leave on Monday?

Yes! I called back. Then came reality. How would I ever make it in time? Bellagio's New York office was sending me a packet of information by express mail. I had to arrange with the library for leave, pay my mortgage and other bills, and call the agent at Cape

Cod who was handling the sale of my place there to notify him of my whereabouts in Italy should there be an offer and he had to be in touch with me. And I was still correcting the galleys of my *Aldus* book! On the day of departure, my last chores and packing done, I almost missed out when an artist friend, lost in his work, forgot to pick me up for the drive to the airport.

I made the flight to Milan. In the air I thought of my second daughter, Susanna, who had been born there in a sultry and oppressive July, and, having breathed her first air in Italy, has made it her home. While awaiting the birth I had seen an ad in the magazine *Grazia* for a rental at Bellagio on Lake Como and suggested to my husband Antonio that we take the place and spend a month on the lake after the baby was born. As it turned out, we did have a month at a lake, but it wasn't Como; it was grim, gray Lake Oneida outside my hometown, Syracuse, New York. My parents wanted to see the new babe and her two-year-old sister and invited us over to stay with them on the lake.

Life is full of chance correspondences. So many years after Susi's birth I, now widowed, was about to have my month at Bellagio after all. And a flowering of ideas for stories began to sprout, wanting to be written.

Yet, once on the plane—quite empty, thankfully—I stretched out across the adjoining empty seats to collapse with the emotional and physical fatigue of the forced march of the past few days. As I dozed off I thought of Cynthia Ozick who, in spidery handwriting on a postcard, had once queried me, Why don't you apply for Bellagio? She and I have had a tiny, occasional correspondence about authorship for over two decades following my interview of her for a Westchester magazine. She is always gracious, concerned, encouraging and with a surprising and equalizing acceptance of me, unknown in the wider world, as a fellow writer. She, of course, had been to Bellagio, has had her MacArthur, her Guggenheim; she writes her novels and other works and hands them to her agent of four decades who sends them off to Knopf her forever publisher, and, *ecco, fatto!* She is in print, in collections, on panels, a member of the American Academy of Arts and Letters. She seems to wonder why that is not my procedure. But publishing for me has been a trial of endurance, each book a different publisher, agents who give up on me. I could seem to have no continuity, no reputation. And yet, before I slept, I thought, I am going to be a resident at Villa Serbelloni in Bellagio, and not as an accompanying wife to Antonio the poet but as myself, author. Happy accidents, too, are part of life, Aristotle observed. I believe it.

At Malpensa airport I am met by the driver from the Bellagio Center who whisks me off in the misty morning toward Lake Como in a strange phantasmagoria of images—dream shreds of imagining myself an Italian signora in a villa, memories of my past life in Italy before Antonio died, my new plans. They all shifted in and out of my half-wake, half-doze state along with those sonorous opening lines of Alessandro Manzoni's *I promessi sposi: "Quel ramo del lago di Como che si svolge verso il mezzogiorno."* (That branch of Lake Como that turns off to the south . . .). Antonio had intoned it long ago, reading the whole of that great novel to me in Italian as I awaited the birth of our first child. Now, along the roadway I actually glimpse a furniture showroom called *I promessi sposi* (The Betrothed), and a Hotel Don Abbondio, named, strangely, for the pavid priest in the novel.

Arriving at Villa Serbelloni I'm greeted by Jackie Sutton, the acting director's wife, and shown my quarters, a palatial room and luxurious bathroom embellished with handcrafted ceramic tiles, custom-made, I'm told. She leaves, I fall into bed and sleep. When I awake and look around, I see a smaller version of a cabriole-legged Venetian dressing table I once owned, the same faded green lacquer and floral decor—it's a remembrance of times past when Antonio and I lived in Rome and I dressed almost nightly to go to some gathering or other. My room is a large chamber with the bed alcove in crimson damask demarcated from the sitting area by a wide archway; French doors open to a balcony that looks upon a scene of incredible pleasure. On the hills in the far view, villas emerge—tawny yellow, rose, cream, buff, all set off by vegetation in differing hues of green. I drink in blue and beautiful Lake Como from on high, seeing it shine in the sunlight, ringed by snow-topped mountains and sprouting little villages on its shoreline. Boats dart over its surface like dragonflies, water beetles. It's Paradise (even though, as I'll later learn, an actual town called Paradiso exists elsewhere on Lake Como, for I'll see it posted as a stop on bus signs and the boat schedule and think, Imagine living there.)

Later I'm shown to my work space down near the lakeside. Jackie Sutton unlocks the door to a room atop an old chapel dedicated to the Madonna of Monserrat and I look upon the delicious space of a white-walled, brick-floored room with two long gothic windows overlooking the lake. "This place is for writers," she tells me. The scholars have more prosaic studios. Framing the green heights of the mountains which plunge to the lake, my windows open to breezes rustling the trees and to a lush growth of poppies, ginestra, wild orchids, correopsis, camomile daisies growing out of walls, and roses climbing everywhere. The room has a table-desk with an IBM electric typewriter, some chairs, and a cupboard holding paper and other supplies. Graffiti from former occupants are scratched on a wall and among them I see Justin Kaplan, Toby Olson. Eventually I add mine: *HB in Paradiso ritrovato.*

Every day, walking through the gardens and grounds from the Villa to my studio, I do traverse paradise. Passing above meadows being mown, or olive trees and grapevines, I see my beautiful Italy of earlier times. And I stop at a view, stunning and revelatory, from the promontory on which the villa is situated above the icy blue of Lake Como. Spread below me and ringed by the Alps, Lake

Como branches into two arms: Lake Lecco to the east, and the continuation of Como to the west. That view becomes emblematic, the very image of duality made visible, perceptible: the pattern of my life and work is made strikingly clear as I see in the lakes the main body of who I am, American, on one side, the Italian on the other, as they flow into each other. From these two confluences am I and my writing formed. My vision from the central height is of division and unity. It's not a question of choice—both realities are simply there. They are divergent, they are one. My straddling position can be none other than that of the Italian American. And it's as Baudelaire said, correspondences are everywhere, we walk through a world of symbols. I feel as if I have already achieved something at Bellagio just by claiming that view.

My day begins with breakfast, not spare Italian-style but abundantly American and with special-order, superb cappuccino to replace regular coffee; there follows a midday coffee break, aperitifs before lunch, tea in the afternoon, another gathering before dinner for cocktails, and finally after-dinner drinks in the sitting room. One is requested to attend all meals, while the in-betweens are by choice. The formal dining room, used when conferees are present, is large enough for two tables of twenty-two persons each. The room has formal sideboards holding elaborate Chinese vases, a Venetian glass chandelier descending from the stucco-adorned ceiling, French doors opening onto the flowering terrace. We usually gather for meals in the smaller dining room, or in good weather on the terrace.

People arrive and depart each week on staggered, scheduled stays so that we have an opportunity to meet many residents, and there are twenty-five to thirty of us in residence at any time. At dinner my first night, I meet the poet Amy Clampitt, the only resident whose name I recognize, and she's due to leave in the morning. I tell her I recently read her "Margaret Fuller" poem and how much I liked it and have always admired Fuller as a feminist precursor. But Clampitt will have none of what she terms feminist nonsense. I learn later that Clampitt's first book didn't come out until she was sixty-three.

Except for me, everyone is affiliated with a university and is thus identifiable. The deceased person I am replacing was a philosopher from Stanford and there are other philosophers here who were acquainted with him. An article once described Villa Serbelloni as "that Plato-haunted, Rockefeller-funded thinkers' retreat on Lake Como" where "grand philosophers may still be found, in a state of postmodern perplexity." When I'm asked what my field is, I want to say, "no field, only views," but am reticent.

Then I am distressed to learn that we were expected to bring with us copies of our published work for display in the library. In the rush of my departure, this was not conveyed to me by the New York office and so there I am, empty-handed with no proof that I belong. All I have is a bilingual edition of Antonio's Italian poems with my English translation that I intended to give to my daughter Susi, but must now leave on the library table, my only shadowy mark. I am aware, too, of all the couples—an invited resident is allowed to be accompanied by spouse or significant other. Paradise is not for singles. The very word imagines a pair, as they were in Eden.

There is table talk of some of the greats who have been here: Leon Edel, Henry James's biographer, is one, leading me to think of Henry and my tie with him because of my Syracuse girlhood home on James Street, named for his grandfather, and also because of Henry's love for Italy and his *Italian Hours* which I will eventually echo in my later collection of stories, *More Italian Hours*. We dine that evening on manicotti with a spinach-cheese filling, poached salmon with a vinaigrette julienne of cucumber on salad greens, crêpes à l'orange, wines and grappa and I hear that we will be expected to give a "fireside chat" of our work during our stay and a farewell speech before we leave.

Following dinner there is a climatology presentation; in addition to the Villa residents, there are often participants of scheduled conferences and tonight is a wrap-up by the climate scientists. Richard Merelman, a personable historian and his wife, sit next to me. "We," he waves his hand to include the Villa residents in the audience, "are nonconsequential in comparison to the climatologists." Yet, I think, the climatologists came to no conclusion about global warming whereas novelists, at least, pin down some enduring, recognizable human state and consequence. I tell Merelman that I feel like an outsider in such company. He says you're not an outsider; no one here is.

Climate reminds me that it's chilly and I have packed the wrong clothes. I should have found out about weather on Lake Como in early June—now I'll have to buy a sweater to keep warm. Still, to be in surroundings of such perfect taste in the understated Italian way; to be treated so elegantly; to be able to stretch out on a chaise after lunch; to have bottled water always there and chamber maids attentive to one's every want, leaving wafers, flowers; to hear, while dining well with fine wines, how David Lodge, a reserved man who only lets go in his novels, was here and then wrote *Small World* about the Bellagio crowd; or how George Kennan, one evening, said that history is not what happened . . . History is what it felt like to be there when it happened (yes, yes, I think to myself, Virginia Woolf kept asking, what did it *feel* like . . .) all this was my long-ago vision of life in Italy.

I ease into the routine of Villa Serballoni life, going early to work and trying to overcome the blank white pages and the unfamiliar typewriter that puts me at great disadvantage because I can't see the line I'm typing, only the one above. The first morning I spend only an hour and a half at work before I quit and walk down the winding stairway to the village of Bellagio where, Swiss-like, the shopkeepers are sweeping their entrances. Everything is clean, orderly and the shops are full of elegant, costly stuff—a tourist-attraction-place like Taormina. I wonder: shall I buy a sweater to keep warm or a camera? I decide for the sweater and to make up for no photos I go to the local tourist office and get a Lake Como poster, gratis.

Bill Wang (pronounced Wong), a linguist collaborating with Luca Cavalli-Sforza (whose "Quest for the Mother Tongue," is featured in the April issue of *Atlantic Monthly* magazine) is reading one of the copies of *I promessi sposi* from the Villa library, and I the other. He's interested in aspects of Italian grammar; why, he asks me, are *Lei*, a form of courteous address and the third person pronoun *lei*, homonyms. Actually they are the same word, and I am pleased to be taken for a serious person. He asks to see where I work and asks about my husband.

"He died some years ago," I say.

"Oh, so you came here as some connection with his work because he was Italian?"

"No. I'm here for myself."

I call Susi in Urbino and tell her all about the Villa and she says, "Yeah, yeah, Mom, that's good—you're with a lot of interesting people!" She says she'll try to get away at the end of the month to come visit me. She has an interesting mishearing of Bellagio as Pelagio, bringing to my mind the Pelagian heresy: the negation of belief in original sin while believing in free will and our ability to choose between good and evil. Yes, for the Pelagians, I tell myself.

My walks are up and down the steep S-curved stairway to the village, all over the grounds finding the follies and following trails. I go up to the Castle Keep, the site of the original fortification that stood on this promontory until the Visconti lords had it razed in the fourteenth century. I pass the 700-year-old oak that, I heard at dinner talk, has just had a thousand-dollar treatment. Mowing the meadows three times a year costs $10,000. The place is enormously expensive to run—a million dollars a year? queries one fellow. More like two- to two-and-a-half million, the director replies. Three of the waiters are from Sri-Lanka because Italian union rules make hiring Italians so costly.

The Rockefeller Foundation received Villa Serbelloni from its last owner, the Detroit-born Ella Walker, heiress of the Hiram Walker Liquors fortune, who married an Italian prince and became Principessa della Torre e Tasso. She was born in 1875 and acquired the property in 1928. There is a charming painting of her in the library showing an elegant, wasp-waisted young lady in Victorian garb—a gleaming mauve-grey ruffled outfit topped by a huge black-plumed hat. She is looking pensively off into the distance, perhaps to America from whence came the pretty penny to run the place beautifully and a lot more extravagantly than in Pliny the Younger's time. For I had found him, too, a seated statue on whose base was inscribed *Hic tragedia, Marcus Plinius, Junior*, in a little shelter off the pathway. Pliny's sculpted face is worn and he looks Zeus-like with his beard; there are scrolls in a bucket by his side and a closed book in his left hand; someone has picked a field daisy and put it in his raised and clenched right fist. He had two places on Lake Como and wrote: "One is set high on a cliff . . . and overlooks the lake. . . . Supported by rock, as if by the stilt-like shoes of the actors in tragedy, I call it Tragedia. It enjoys a broad view of the lake which the ridge on which it stands divides in two. . . ." That is my view, too. I am glad to have found him.

When it rains and gets foggy, the view across the lake is completely lost. Fearing my workspace will be clammy, I then stay in my room, read, think, and make notes. I think of Margaret Fuller, one of the women of my work-in-the-making to whom Italy was revelatory. Fuller is one of my great heroes, and she was here in

August 1847 when she made the momentous decision not to return home to the States with her American traveling companions but to remain in Italy. She toured north Italy by herself and in Milan she met Manzoni and others interested in the Italian independence movement.

"I am alone here," she wrote to a friend at home, "alone with glorious Italy. . . . Imagine if I do not enjoy being here, in 'Bellagio's woods.' The life here on the lake is precisely what we once at Newbury imagined. . . ."

And poor, doomed Roderick Hudson, the hero of Henry James's novel of the same name who came to such a tragic end, had his last few days at Lake Como where, he agreed with his fellow travelers, "it was the earthly paradise." It is in this novel that the Princess Casamassima, who enthralled Roderick, is introduced. She is a fascinating character, born Christina Light in Italy of an Italian father and American mother, hence, Italian American in the way my own daughters are. Knowing he cannot, Roderick tormentedly asks, "Why not stay here forever?" Because even then, James his creator observed, it's the Italy one has ceased to believe in.

But I, not Henry, am here for a month, and I believe it all.

When it rains, there are furled white umbrellas in a large amphora near the front entrance for us to use. I take one and slog through the mud to visit the settlement below the villa and then go on to Bellagio to shop but everything's expensive and I consider that it would be worthwhile to take the bus into Como for the Saturday market. Many of the wives accompanying their scholar husbands spend their time going to Como to shop for its renowned silk goods—scarves, neckties, and such. I fret about having the wrong wardrobe, especially at dinner when I see Jackie Sutton, always perfectly coiffed and turned out in handsome evening outfits.

Some evenings there are fireside chats, informal discussions of their work by the residents. One of the accompanying wives says to me: You are the mystery woman here, no one knows what you're doing. And I wonder, does she really mean, no one knows what you're doing here? But it's natural no one knows me—I arrived with no books, articles, or academic title and affiliation, not even a press release for my forthcoming *Aldus* to put on display in the library. Just me. In the wrong clothes. And my hair needs doing. When I talk to Susi and tell her I'm the mystery person here, she says, "Good, Mom, that's a position of power." She is married to an Italian and has lived in Italy for so many years that I sometimes think we have a language problem.

I converse with poet John Engels. I tell him I saw his book of poetry on the library table and very much liked reading his poem, "Vivaldi, in the Fall." And then it turns out he's never been to Venice to hear Vivaldi's work played in his own church, La Pietà. A charming Iranian woman who has accompanied her professor-husband speaks to me of her Persian cookbook that came out with the University Press of Virginia and of which she is passionately proud and I tell her my Italy memoir *Festa* is also a cookbook. I am flooded with remembrances of my past life. I think of Lucretius, whose *De rerum natura* I read long ago in college, and the passage, "So, little by little, time brings out each several thing into view, and reason raises it up onto the shores of light." That gives me "Shores of Light," as the title for a story I'm thinking out.

New people arrive, among them a friendly American, Donna Merrick, and her more remote Australian husband Greg Dening, both historians, both formerly in the Catholic clergy, she a nun and he a priest. I learn from others just by being here, listening to them, and reading their work: Greg Dening's explication of Irony in History, for instance, in his stunning book, *Mr. Bligh's Bad Language: Passion, Power and Theatre on the Bounty*, shows him a fine writer.

We are in the realm of Teodolinda, the medieval Queen of the Lombards, for whom my first child is named. I take the boat across the lake to Varenna but once there skip the hard climb above town to the remains of the castle-rock that was Teodolinda's last residence. Instead, I send a postcard to my daughter and buy her a commemorative dish towel with the supposed likeness of her namesake. We are also near Val Camonica, where I once journeyed with Antonio to Capo di Ponte to see the prehistoric petroglyphs, newly discovered rock carvings. Also nearby is Dongo where Mussolini, trying to flee Italy in the last days of the war, was captured along with his mistress; and I think of Stendahl naming his hero of *The Charterhouse of Parma* Fabrizio del Dongo and having him be born in a villa on Lake Como.

Quite incredible for me in this bucolic setting is the sighting of a plaque at the Hotel Splendide in the village that notes that the futurist poet Filippo Tommaso Marinetti died there on December 2, 1944 (*Poeta futurista qui morì*). Here, indeed, is Greg Dening's irony in history. Marinetti was the poet of fascist force and might, the extoller of the dynamism of modern life, of violence as an affirmation of individuality, and of war as manly exercise. And yet he spent the war years in this sheltered spot on Lake Como, far from the thrilling battle and bombardments of his bellicose words.

It is pleasant to walk in town with the townspeople out for their *passeggiata*. Well-dressed and well-fed, they belch aloud, eat ice cream endlessly, stroll and chat, head one way to Punta Spartivento that juts out into the lake, then turn and walk in the opposite direction. I have with me Greg Dening's book on the Bounty, a truly remarkable example of ethnographic history that is seductive by virtue of his style and eloquence. He helps me see myself, as novelist of a particular group whose behavior and environment I interpret as a kind of accidental ethnographer, interested in the phenomenon of "otherness," in the ambivalence which is created in people with dual cultures to draw upon. I wrote it uncon-sciously in *Umbertina* (about Italians coming to America), and now Greg Dening gives it a precise context. In fact a future novel of mine will again be about displacement, but in the other direc-tion—an American transplant in Italy. After a week in residence I try to sum up what I've done: notes and revisions for several stories, my work on the women. A lot of reading. Visions. But what brought me here—to start the novel—is still in the wings.

A new conference is scheduled on the theme of the 1941 Ger-man invasion of Russia, a fifty-year commemorative. As custom-ary, the conferees mingle with us residents at dinner. I sit next to a Russian who teaches at Harvard, quotes Cicero, and says, "Are you here alone, if I may ask?" He says he's philosophic because deficient in other areas. When he asks what books I write, I hesi-tate, then say, they're about displacement. He replies, I prefer love stories. Then, unsettlingly, he says, "You are secretive . . . you have an invisible life." Yes, I tell him, it's my Sicilian heritage, plus being born under the sign of Scorpio.

On, June 13th, the feast of Sant'Antonio, I take the day off to go with the Canadian couple to see the renowned Thyssen art collec-tion at Villa Favorita in Lugano. And it is full of wonderful things including Ghirlandaio's splendid portrait in profile of the twenty-year-old Florentine beauty, Giovanna Tornabuoni, justly re-nowned as one of the most beautiful portraits of the Quattrocento. It is a likeness I have grown familiar with, for it hangs as a poster in my Montserrat work space. I also see the Taddeo Gaddi nativity scene, so familiar to me from the copy that hung in my childhood home.

When Donna Merwick says, "Helen, why don't you give a fire-side chat?" I tell her I could if some of my material arrives. Or maybe, I add, I can do it just on the effect she and Greg have had on me through their talks and writings. "No, a talk on method would not be interesting," says Greg, "people here talk substance." I think of myself as a Greg Dening "beachcomber" (a term he uses in his *Islands and Beaches*), from my not having yet successfully mediated in life and work between my two cultures. And then I realize with a start how appropriate "beachcomber" is to the character Marguerite in my novel *Umbertina*; caught between two worlds and unable to secure sure footing in either, she actually asks herself the vital question, "But what world is there that's not beached first in ourselves?" In any case, just to be prepared, I start writing out some thoughts on creativity at Bellagio and, of course, my vision of the lake's division into two branches is the operative metaphor.

One evening there is a brief flurry of excitement around me when I get a fax delivered to me in the lounge after dinner. It is an offer on my place at the Cape for my full asking price. People are interested—they can't figure out what I'm doing here, but this real estate transaction gives me substance, a presence in the real world of business affairs.

Being at Bellagio is my open sesame for a veritable onslaught of memory. I observe, reflect, remember: a parade of scenes, people, places. The creative process is errant, vagabond, unpredictable. Plans change, the process evolves. My novel becomes something else. And the story, "Shores of Light," is having interesting ramifications around the theme of the Anglo-American "possession" of Italy as their prime material even as I adjust it to my Italian American view.

When I depict a heroine living in Italy she will be different from past characters: an American, born and raised in the United States who is of Italian descent and meets Italy head-on as a pivotal player in her search for an identity that is not the demeaning one she shunned in America. I've learned from historian Donna Merwick who reads early New York State history from Dutch sources, as well as from the sources of the conquering English, in order to get a different story. Through different filters, the story changes. As Greg Dening would say, "a Cliometric moment."

Things change. At breakfast we learn that in the outside world, by popular referendum, Leningrad has become St. Petersburg once again. And Natale, the head butler, actually observes to one of the professors that gentlemen don't point. I wonder why we are still having winter fruit—apples, pears, or oranges—when the shops in town are full of peaches, apricots, figs, melons, berries. Even here on the grounds there are cherry trees, laden with fruit waiting to be picked. Then at lunch, following delicious green gnocchi with gorgonzola sauce and a gorgeous salad, there are bowls of peaches and I hear the director ask, "Do I dare to eat a peach?"

That afternoon, on a walk down to the Sfrondata Tower, I see among the cherry trees a scene that looks taken from a *Book of Hours*: two women are gathering cherries, one in a cherry tree with an old-time wicker basket on her arm, the other bracing a ladder against the tree. It's a charming picture and now I regret that I bought a sweater instead of a camera.

Meron Benvenisti has arrived from Israel and brought his works. I have been reading his *Conflicts and Contradictions*, a beautifully written, and finally compassionate, understanding of the Israeli-Palestinian conflict. When I compliment him, he modestly claims that the use of "I" in his writing is laziness—it saves him from having to do research, check facts, look for material: all his material is his own opinion. Yet his voice is one that I can well hear and respect: ". . . through our ambivalence we represent both the bond to the past and the break with it . . . By sharing with my children my contradictions, I bequeath the human values I inherited." But then he says, "I suffer from an almost permanent sense of dissonance . . . the personal feeling of inadequacy . . . left in me a deep emotional scar that has never really healed. . . . Israeli Jews can't make over the Diaspora Jews to their image—

even in the Chosen there is separateness." Reading him I understand how the universal sense of separateness afflicts and infests everyone, yet how the Yoga message of oneness could redeem us all. Benvenisti has the moral commitment of the old Zionist ideals—Israel as a democracy, not a state of a dominant majority oppressing a minority. But how achieve it?

Some days it rains off and on. At first all is clear, then it pours; the pouring abates, the mist lifts and it's clear again, then it pours. Inspired by the rain, Alba Cavalli-Sforza gives us her translation of D'Annunzio's poem, *La pioggia nel pineta* (Rain in the Pine Forest), and as she reads I hear echoes of Joyce's marvelous, moving finale to his story "The Dead." Then I wonder, did he absorb that cadence of falling rain from D'Annunzio and turn it into the snow falling here and there and everywhere over tombstones and being general all over Ireland? I think also of another beautiful D'Annunzio poem that begins, "*È settembre* . . . and is about the shepherds in September moving their sheep down from summer mountain pastures of the Abruzzi. D'Annunzio has been downgraded for his florid verse and flamboyant mode of living, but he remains a poet—if only for those two poems. The rainstorms have caused a lot of debris from tree branches to fall on the lake and the once dazzling blue waters now have a brown scum floating over them along the shore.

At Prof. Donaldson's fireside chat he begins his talk on Truth with a quote from Jean Rhys. Then I am called away to the telephone to speak to lawyer Cavanaugh on Cape Cod who says I have a deal—he will fax me the new offer incorporating my provisions. That's good news and after hearing the remainder of Donaldson's talk, I am buoyed up enough to tell him I'm glad he started a talk on truth with a quote from a novelist, thus elevating fiction which gives us emotional truth. That's a postmodernist comment, Donna observes, though it's news to me. She and Greg are open to imaginative, open-ended ruminations and quite weary of the endless, heavy-footed, earnest search for Truth and who'll get to it first as if it were the South Pole.

I am feeling the good effects of being with diverse people from all over, and realize that I have been too much alone. Italy speaks to me in the order and harmony of the landscape, the civility of the people, a prevailing sense of humane, unforced, decorum—those very shores of light I have to beach. In the evening, on my balcony just as dusk has softened everything but it is all still vaguely visible and lights are just starting to come on and be reflected in the lake, I feel the beauty and am elated to receive it.

Sometimes, though, what I feel is being out of step. I do not dress au courant like the accompanying women in miniskirts, sarongs, and tank tops; I don't wear serpent earrings down to my shoulders, or have a Vidal Sassoon haircut. I had my fashionable period when I was a signora in Rome. Here I am peculiarly foreign. Maybe the trouble lies in my not hewing the straight and narrow line of specialization. If I had become a professional of a subject, that would have given me definition, security, tenure, a network of fellow practitioners, and an exchange of recommendations for all the hospitable places that put up professors during vacation months and sabbatical years. And who do they study and write and talk about? Obscure novelists, or Wittgenstein, say, the solitary hermetic iconoclast and deflator of all they honor; or mutineers and beachcombers; the "Others" of society and literature. The loners and non-joiner amateurs are the meat and potatoes of the academic world. And so maybe that's it—my role, as that of all writers, is just to be the *materia prima*.

The Cavalli-Sforzas are going to Lugano and suggest I join them. Alba Cavalli-Sforza and I have already reminisced about Italy's first postwar scandal that occurred at the luxurious Hotel Villa d'Este on Lake Como not far from where we actually are. I was coming into Italy for the first time and had bought my first Italian news magazine, attracted by the cover photo of a bejeweled woman in evening dress with cold, brooding eyes under the screaming headline, *Delitto di passione!* (crime of passion). The woman was Countess Pia Bellantani, shown attending a ball with her husband at the hotel where she shot and killed her war-profiteer lover. And Alba correctly observes that the real scandal was the incredible exhibit of *la bella gente* in full regalia in luxurious surroundings enjoying themselves with fine food, service, all the trappings, and dressed to the nines in the immediate postwar period when all Italy, bombed and depleted, was struggling to get by. It was certainly a revelation to me who had just come from England where food was still rationed and people were decently shabby. I could never have imagined the contrast to high life at the Villa d'Este, as if there had been no Italian defeat, no privations and general *miseria*, no more pressing needs in the Countess's egocentric life than to get rid of a loutish lover.

But I decline going to Lugano again and go, instead, by boat with the British couple to Gravidona, near Dongo, on a delta that gives it more flat area than most lakeshore towns. Bypassing it is the Via Regia (changed into Regina by local usage and thus a wrong attribution to Queen Teodolinda) that connects Como to the northern passes and would have been the route for Mussolini's escape from Italy. We saw an impressive early church called S. Maria del Tiglio (St. Mary of the Lindentree), completed by the master builders of Como in the twelfth century with carved stonework on the facade taken from an even earlier structure.

Greg and Donna, perhaps because of their past religious offices, invite me to attend mass with them, which I haven't done in years, and I am gratified to see a young girl in vestments serving at the altar with the priest. A copy of my novel has finally been sent to me by Susi, and Donna is reading it. Then Susi calls and says she will be arriving at the end of the month. I meet her in Como and take her to lunch—48,000 lire for *crespelle* and salad! We visit the Cathedral, the art collection of the Pinocoteca, and

Standa, the Italian version of an old-time Woolworth's ten-cent store now sadly gone from American life. We admire a certain Ico Parisi's sculpture in the main piazza—a car emerging from a huge stone block. That evening Susi and I walk down from the villa to Pescolo and we eat under a vined trellis overlooking the lake. Then we go back up the steep hill to the Villa for the concert that's been planned for the evening and have strawberry tarts at intermission.

Susi, speaking of her husband, describes him as *titubante*, hesitant, anxious—and gives me a new word that I immediately know I will use in "Shores of Light." That's my acquired word on this journey, although "claptrap" frequently comes to mind. Susi is at ease in making conversation with the scholars; she tells me how well Donna speaks of me—saying how human and accessible I am, not at all full of airs and pretensions like some of the others. Then Susi's visit is over and on Sunday morning we take the 7:20 A.M. boat for Varenna so that Susi can make the Milan connection and be home in the afternoon. I tell her I won't be staying over in Italy after my month at Bellagio is up because of the pending Cape Cod sale. I will leave earlier than I planned.

Since June 21st, the first day of summer, the weather has been beautiful. We dine on the terrace, gather there in the evening and watch lights appear on the mountains, the moon come up over the lake. Everything turns to shades of blue with an orange path over Lake Lecco from the almost full and tawny moon. It's dusk until 9:45 or so and I think of Antonio's favorite lines from Purgatory, Canto 8 of the *Commedia*: "*Era già l'ora che volge il disio / ai navicanti e 'ntenerisce il cor* ("Now was the hour that wakens fond desire / In men at sea and melts their heart. . . .") How can I plant this view in my head, memorize it, incise it forever? The deep blues of water and mountain, the pale grey-blue mist, the violet-blue clouds, the yellow lights, the blinking light in the Sfondrata Tower, the balminess, the calm. The ferries, white-lighted going, red-lighted coming, and traveling across the water like giant water bugs.

Elena in the Villa office works miracles and changes my ticket so that I can leave July 3rd. I am set to do my talk with Donna Merrick as a dialogue between us on "Narrative Constructions." Donna, the historian, will examine history as narrative by reading place and documentation as text; I, the novelist, will present narrative as history by telling the story of an immigrant family.

Part of the farewell ritual, along with the fireside chat and a final thank-you toast, is the photo opportunity: we can choose a spot anywhere in villa or on the grounds to be photographed. I would like to be on the promontory with the backdrop of the two branches of Lake Como, but it's not possible to shoot that view so I settle for standing on the grand outdoor stone stairway flanked by hunt sculpture. In large albums in the reading room can be found the photos and descriptions of past residents into which I will soon be inducted.

The weather is hot and humid now. People are edgier and almost obviously divided between Israeli supporters and those who object to United States intervention and the Gulf War. Always appealing, on the other hand, is scientist Lynn Margulies who lives in Amherst near Emily Dickenson's homestead and knows her poems by heart. Lynn tells me something extraordinary: though her husband Ricardo is in Barcelona, she's never been lonely, doesn't even know what the emotion feels like. The nearest she came to understanding it was in her previous marriage (and that, I discover much later, was to the celebrated astronomer Carl Sagan). I think she is the closest to genius that this place has at the moment—her intensity, her projecting voice, her zeal for her work on spirochytes, her fearlessness in swimming in the cold lake, her reservoir of Dickinson committed to memory. And I tell her how Emily's #80 is the theme in my profiles of six American women and their connection to Italy.

Donna Merwick and I give our presentation. For us both, the point is that the past is not reality until we reclaim it and its symbols into the present and understand the Other. I read from *Umbertina* and Donna from her work-in-progress, *The Remarkable Writers of New Netherland*. Francis Sutton says our duet was unique and very successful, and I am grateful to Donna for initiating it. A large photo of a white-haired Princess Ella della Torre e Tasso smiles benevolently at us and the other recipients of her largesse. I admire her vision, making accessible to so many people from so many lands this beautiful space and time for work and meetings. The seat of her husband's title was the Castle of Duino, outside Trieste, famous for Rilke's *Duino Elegies*, and she was buried there when she died in 1959, just ten days after completing the will in which she bequeathed Villa Serbelloni to the Rockefeller Foundation as a scholarly residence and conference site, along with an endowment of two million dollars. She had no heirs; how better use her fortune?

The day before my departure I finally take the bus to Lecco for a Manzoni itinerary. The town is entered by a fourteenth-century bridge erected by the Visconti lords and the stop is at the main square dominated by a statue of Alessandro Manzoni. A tiny area of Lecco is known as Pescarenico and still looks as it did when Manzoni described the seventeenth-century setting of his novel— the narrow streets, habitations crowded together around courtyards piled high with kindling wood, and the miniscule Piazza dei Pescatori (Fishermen Square) where even today nets dry along the lakeshore. There are signs indicating the *Itinerario Manzoniano* and I follow them, glad to see the convent where Lucia was given hospitality after her flight and wishing that Antonio and I had done this itinerary together when we lived in Milan so close by and he was reading the novel aloud to me.

I get back from Lecco in time to go down to my workroom and type out notes for my farewell speech in the evening. Then I have to pack. This last time, going down to dinner, I stand for some moments on the great stairway, looking straight down the splendid hall to the arched glass door at the opposite end leading to the graveled terrace; Francis Sutton is playing the piano in the music room. It's all lovely. And I think with gratitude of what this stay in the Villa has been for me—the ideas and exchange it has given me, the stories to write, the people I've met. My bounty.

I should not have had the aperatifs plus so much wine at dinner, for I forget many of my lines when I give my farewell speech. I want to say, "Let me count the ways,"—the ways this stay has been so fruitful and memorable. It comes out differently, but somehow I get through, telling of the image of the lake split into two branches even as I straddle two worlds; recalling how, after Susi was born, I first wanted to reach Bellagio but hadn't until now. Aferwards, Linda Kerber comes up and says, "A real class act." And Donna adds, "That's just what I'm going to do—what Helen did." I'm amazed.

And then I'm home. Just a few weeks after returning, the travel section of the *New York Times* has an interesting insert about the ultimate splurge to pamper yourself: a week's stay at the Hotel Villa d'Este on Lake Como for a cost of $5,385.00. Applying that figure to my own four-week stay at Villa Serballoni, my bill would have amounted to almost $22,000.00. But I had more than a luxury splurge. I worked at my work in the special company of scholars and artists, beached my shores of light, and found an image of identity to last me as long as memory.

III   Return

Shutting the Door on Someone

It's been a long time since I've cared to remember the day I shut the front door of our Croton house in John Cheever's face. My weird response to his ring and to seeing him on our porch, dwarfed by the columns of that large, four-square grey stucco house, so dismayed me at the time that I chose to obliterate it. I never mentioned it to anyone. Nor did I ever refer to it on any occasion I ever saw John again, not to apologize, not to explain, not even to laugh it off as I might have since he was forever amused and indulgent at the bizarreness of everything.

And so I have never known what he thought as the door closed. Did he imagine that I might have been sheltering the FedEx man? That I was batty? A prude? Maybe he was wise enough to see a young woman thoroughly discomfited and taken aback by the unexpected presence of a well-known writer saying, "I've brought back your stories," as he held out a thick manila envelope. He had driven over from Scarborough to give me the packet. I gasped, "Oh!" said "Thank you," and immediately shut the door.

I panicked. I was not only taken by surprise, I was also terrified by what John might have said. In a colossal failure of nerve, and in a split second, it must have flashed through my mind that he could—politely, of course—dismiss the stories, wipe out what confidence was burgeoning, turn off those tentative beginnings of mine. He might have said something like, "Look, if you have any-thing better to do, why don't you." He might, on the other hand, have said "I think these show promise." But at that point in my life, having receded into the shadowy recesses of translating my husband's stories and camouflaging my voice with his, my hold on my own work was too fragile to risk losing through any words that might have pushed me further into the morass of self-doubt.

All this occurred at mid-morning on a fall day years ago after we first met the Cheevers, and just before we moved from the stucco house in Croton to the barn house we purchased from Aaron Copland at Shady Lane Farm in Ossining Town. I still remember the acrid odor of faded, once-blooming geraniums from the boxes on the front porch in Croton that hit my nostrils when I opened the door. It was the end of summer; sun and light were lower on the earth. There must have been a chill—perhaps a frost?—John was wearing a camel's hair coat. I was alone at home since my husband had gone off to his office in New York on the commuters' 8:02 from Croton-Harmon as usual; and our two girls were at school. It was because they were enrolled at Scarborough Country Day School that we met the Cheevers. Ginny Kahn, who was then married to E. J. Kahn Jr., long of *The New Yorker*, was at a parents' function Antonio and I attended. The minute we were introduced to the Kahns and Antonio opened his mouth, Ginny exclaimed, "You're Italian!" followed by, "You'll have to meet the Cheevers who've just come back from Italy." And so we did. And, in a strange conjunction, when we moved into the Copland house, John and Mary Cheever were about to move into their own new home just over the hill from us, which made us neighbors.

In many ways John and Antonio had similar natures. They both had a natural gentleness and fragility from privation in boyhood—Antonio had lost his father, a naval officer when he was only nine and John's New England family had begun coming apart when he, too, was young and susceptible. Both had genteel families who had seen better days. Both were natural and hilarious storytellers who embellished deft embroideries on the stories they told. They were also both very religious, and haunted by loss. They communicated in versions of either English or Italian depending on who was using which language. They enjoyed each other's company, and there was that counterpart of Antonio's ongoing discovery of America and John's just having been in Italy that bound them. At the same time they were worlds apart and John's suburbia was never Antonio's provinces or vice versa.

John had just published *The Wapshot Chronicle*. Ever since my girlhood in upstate New York, I had been reading his stories in *The New Yorker*. Now Antonio's stories, in my translation, were also appearing in *The New Yorker*. He was pleased, but much less taken by the aura of that publication and of John's name than I was. He simply delighted in the company of meeting an American author who had just come back, enthusiastic, from his country.

So many strands go into this story! The telling of it is not just my overwrought and inconsiderate action in closing the door on John Cheever, but all the factors and events that led up to it: from my growing up in an Italian American family in Syracuse to my nourishing, as long as I can remember, an unconfessed and guilty wish to be a writer as were those men and women I revered and whose works I lugged home every Saturday, after confession at the Blessed Sacrament, when I stopped at the Eastwood branch of the public library. How did I, from a family who did not love books, become enamored of the written word? Was it the beautiful fairy tale book my father once brought me back from a business trip to Chicago perhaps on the suggestion of a salesperson when he was searching for a gift? Or was it something in school that caught me and led me, ever after, to library after library? Something took hold of me and by high school I had a subscription to *The New Yorker* which, when it arrived, was the highlight of the week for me as *Life* magazine was for my two brothers.

I seemed to be the only student at the Convent School of the Franciscan Sisters Motherhouse in Syracuse who knew and admired those far-away people named John Cheever, John O'Hara,

Mary McCarthy, E. J. Kahn, Wolcott Gibbs, William Maxwell, Gênet. They were the most luminous names I could think of. They, and not those old standbys—Columbus, Dante, Verdi (always extolled at annual Columbus Day dinners to help the Italian American community feel better about itself, especially in those war years when Italy was an axis power and our enemy)—they, Cheever, and company were the eminences I thought about. To write like that!

I lived a plain, upstate life. My Convent School classmates were simple girls, of Irish or German background, who took piano lessons and were serious about their religion. I lost mine, at age twelve. Though I stopped going to confession I continued to visit the Eastwood branch library. I wanted to read what I couldn't find among the drab and untouched books in our Convent library. What were missing were the forbidden books on the Index and when I found them I wondered why Voltaire's wit and good sense, for instance, seemed so dangerous to the nuns. I was looked upon as a renegade, kept on, despite my attitude, because the Mother Superior had once been my own mother's teacher and one must risk all for the one lost sheep. Still, despite my high grades, despite the English prize and a Regents college scholarship, I was not allowed to be head girl at graduation. Paris may have been worth a Mass to Henry IV of France, but for me the opportunity of giving the valedictory address was not. I said goodbye to my classmates who went on to colleges named for the saints while I went to one named for a businessman: Wells College was endowed with the fortune Henry Wells made with his Wells Fargo express.

At Wells I continued the years of Latin started at the Convent; the light and warmth of the classical world swept over me in all its beauty and composure and I felt the power of the Mediterranean locus of my forebears; it was the lure to an essential part of myself with which I longed to connect. As with the forbidden books (including, effectively, though not specifically, Shakespeare because he was not in our book of Catholic authors), so in my Italian American family, Italy and things Italian were also effectively neglected except for our daily bread. Everything else about Italy was cause for shame and humiliation, like those *March of Time* newsreels featuring Mussolini, the strutting buffoon; the shameful assault on Ethiopia; the treachery against France. It was difficult to live with an Italian name in those days, and, after the war, actually to want to go over and explore my Italian background seemed to my parents—to everybody—like a typical act of contrariness. We came here to get away from Italy, my grandfather had observed.

I got there not knowing Italian because it was not spoken, ever, in my assimilated family. I had a letter of introduction from a graduate school classmate to a journalist named Antonio Barolini in Milan who, perhaps, might help me get around because it was 1948 and conditions were still chaotic. The journalist read me his poetry. I studied Italian. He said he would learn English. I read his first novel, published in 1943 during the height of the war, when only a few hundred copies survived a bombardment and eventually none, since it had been printed on an ersatz paper that was already yellowed and crumbling. Antonio and I married. He said we would have a life of art together, two writers. We married and I soon had three children to care for.

Life's circumstances are unforeseeable. Our first daughter was born in Syracuse, our second in Milan, and the third in Westchester. We were settled in Westchester County in the big old stucco house in Croton about which Antonio wrote a series of poems collected into a volume, called *Elegie di Croton*, that was to win a literary award in Italy. Before that, however, he had already begun to publish quite regularly in *The New Yorker*. His stories, which I loved, were evocations of the prewar Veneto region he grew up in and where his family roots were. I was his translator (never acknowledged in that era of *The New Yorker* with a credit line) and that was the only work of mine I saw in print for a long while. I had the home, the children, the satisfaction of helping my husband and seeing him published in a prestigious magazine—I had even gotten to know John Cheever because I was married to Antonio!

'It should have all been enough. But it wasn't. I was a writer, too. Unpublished but undaunted. I wrote stories, too.

I don't know how John Cheever got my story manuscripts but I have often thought it was Antonio who, sensing my discontent, might have asked John to have a look at them and see if they were publishable. That's what I imagine because I can remember the rage I felt when a surburban woman whose name I have long ago forgotten invited us to dinner and, ingratiatingly, I thought, served chicken tetrazzini which is not an Italian dish but the pasta equivalent of what Wonder Bread is to a freshly baked crusty Italian loaf. Over espresso she produced a sheaf of her own stories with the suggestion that Antonio might introduce her to his editor at *The New Yorker*. I was shocked at her boldness. More, I was frustrated and angry at myself that the years had passed without my becoming a writer in my own right. "We were to be artists together!" I said on the way home as if Antonio, and not I, were responsible for the silence.

All this led up to the morning when John Cheever appeared in Croton with my stories. Why didn't I ask him in for coffee? Why didn't I ask him how he got the stories, what he thought of them? Antonio died without my ever having asked if he had any part in it, as I suspect he did. John is gone now. I think, when I shut the door on him, I must have felt that John would think of me as I did the woman who served chicken tetrazzini and then asked for a favor; he'd think we valued him only for what he might do for me.

But even more, I now realize, it was the moment of total self-illumination in which I repeated to myself that self-chastizing and self-effacing phrase of my convent education, *domine, non sum dignus* correcting it mentally, in the intellectual pride the nuns accused me of, to *domine, non sum digna*. It was not just the Convent School that taught me to efface myself before the male partner who was surely more important, worthier, better. It was also my family education which upheld and passed on the sacrificial position of the woman. We were the uprights of the home; we were there to give of ourselves for our men and for our children. We were not there just for ourselves.

John had his own moments of self-doubt; did he recognize the reflex of my anxiety when I closed the door and so, in charity and graciousness, refrain from ever mentioning the episode to me? That is the only explanation I have for we continued to see the Cheevers until we returned to live in Italy and he never spoke of the incident. Nor did Antonio. Not even when the three of us were together in Antonio's room at the hospital in Sleepy Hollow, where three years earlier our third daughter had been born, and now Antonio was recovering from his first heart attack.

We and the Cheevers were neighbors on lands that had belonged to the Acker brothers in pre-Revolutionary times. John and one of his dogs often walked over the hill and down past our house to the aqueduct trailway which led to Croton Dam. John's *Wapshot Scandal* had followed his first novel and won him the National Book Award. His picture had appeared on the cover of *Time*. He told about being stopped on Main Street of Ossining by a man who looked at him quizzically and said, "Aren't you someone?" No, John answered. "You are someone," said the man, "you're David Wayne the actor."

Antonio's stories had been collected and published in a volume and, again in my translation, Pantheon was to publish his novel with a Cheever endorsement on the book jacket. As for me, I had gone to library school.

When Antonio was stricken, I was the acting director of Briarcliff Manor Public Library and each day I would go from the library to the hospital to visit him. One day I brought him a bright yellowy-orange silk tie. John was in the room when I got there. *Auguri!* I said as I bent over and kissed Antonio. He unwrapped the gift package, beamed, and extended the tie at arm's length to gaze at it: *"Bellissima!"* he smiled. John was amused: "Will you wear that?" he asked Antonio.

"Of course," Antonio said, noticeably cheered. He recognized the augury, knew that it was a symbol of light and the summer to come.

In fact, in the summer after his hospitalization he was back in Italy, looking for a place in Rome where we were to join him while I, saddened, sold the house at Shady Lane Farm and got the children ready for our trip. We lived in Rome for eight years and I began to write there and to see my work published. I started a novel. Just before it was finished Antonio had his second, fatal, heart attack.

I moved back to a small house in Ossining. John and Mary came to see me, and I went to visit them at the lovely old house where they still lived, adjoining Shady Lane Farm. Maybe John had forgotten the shut door. I hadn't.

I think he understood about pain and loneliness and self-doubt and all the self-tormenting things that assail us, even on sunny days and days filled with comely children and a devoted spouse. I think he understood about the longings of the heart, about irrational and eccentric behavior cloaking our fear and terror. I think he knew of the colossal failure of nerve that sometimes comes to all of us. With me it was the mirror side of that unbridled pride that had wafted me through my Convent School years and had taken me to Italy. I think John knew that that door hadn't closed on him as much as it had sheltered me from what, then, I couldn't bear to know.

John is gone now. On occasion when I used to go into New York, I'd stand on the station platform with the late commuters waiting for the 9:37 local. It was always preceded by a fast Amtrak train going in the other direction, north. That fast train had named cars: DeWitt Clinton, Manitoba, James Fenimore Cooper, Hudson Valley . . . and then, there it was, the silver-grey coach named the John Cheever.

Ciao, John, I'd whisper. The car would whiz by, a glimmer of quick recognition and remembrance, then gone in a flash.

Paris in the Boondocks

Not long ago, invited to return to my old college in upstate New York to give a reading, I decided in a fit of romanticism that for the occasion I would wear my mother's honeymoon blouse.

It still hangs in my closet. It is no ordinary blouse. It is cut velvet lined with silk and was acquired in Paris on my parents' honeymoon trip of 1923. The cut velvet is of a leaden gray-green color, between khaki and loden, something like the sheen of spring mud, appliqued over a darker hue of chiffon and thinly banded at the neckline with a strip of bright blue that also shows through the short, slashed sleeves. A full overblouse tightening at the waistband, it is a twenties flapper item that in our own eclectic day seemed newly chic and fashionable. It could have been made to order for a silk skirt I had once bought at a Saks Fifth Avenue winter clearance sale and not yet worn. The blouse would not only solve the problem of my outfit but would also provide a humorous, self-ironic story for my opening remarks.

I jotted down some notes about the blouse as a deliberate choice illustrating a growth process:

1. My early amusement at the idea of the Parisian blouse as part of my mother's wardrobe since she and my father proceeded with it from Paris and Rome to visit their family in deepest, poorest Calabria where their parents had come from.

2. My pride that my mother had such a blouse, on such a honeymoon trip—an accomplishment for a daughter of immigrants. I wanted to be proud of something, growing up as I did in

Syracuse, a very insecure Italian American not really knowing to which part of that duality I belonged. The blouse spoke of American achievement and moneymaking and, more, the taste to spend it in Paris.

3. Nostalgia: returning home to Syracuse from Italy after my Italian husband's death I had come upon the blouse in the attic cedar closet and taken it for my own closet to hang with my outfits from Rome, reminders of another life.

4. Or was it, in both my mother's case and mine, the reminder that neither she, returning from her honeymoon, nor I, settled in Rome with an Italian poet, actually lived out our dreams of fine lives ever after.

Deciding to wear the blouse for my reading at Wells College was, perhaps, the acceptance of all things past, the painful and the pleasurable. I would wear it to put myself figuratively into my mother's skin, to accept her and our differences, recognizing her gifts as well as the limitations which had divided us. I would wear it to honor the mother who, when I was eight or nine, bought me a diary at Emily Mundy's Bookstore now long gone from Syracuse's downtown, and presciently said, "This is to write in." For that's what I did, and have ever since.

Packing the blouse, I drove upstate from where I now live, in a Hudson River village just outside New York City, on a glorious late October day; the recent rains had taken the flame-reds and oranges out of the leaves and left foliage of muted russets, maroon, old gold. I went by way of Ithaca, glimpsing Lake Cayuga, still gently beclouded with morning fog and mist, but shining with a placid prettiness. Then Route 34 took me from the ridge overlooking the lake into farmland, gentle and comfortable with pumpkins on farm porches and roadside stands of apples and honey. I was listening to the voice of nostalgia, playing the cassette tapes of Vladimir Nabokov's *Speak, Memory*, the evocation of his Russian boyhood.

At a crossroads where I had to turn left onto 34B for King Ferry and descend once more to the lake, I came upon an interesting old-fashioned building called the Old Rogue's Inn where I would have liked to stop for coffee, but since it lacked any sign of life I pulled in at Kathy's Corner, on the other side of the road. When I walked in, a waitress (Kathy?) looked at me, silently walked away, and left me to figure out the protocol in the place as she went behind a counter and swiped at it with a cloth, still ignoring me. Finally she looked up. "Black coffee, please," I said. "There," she answered, and jerked her head in the direction of where I had come in. A sign over a thermos jug read, Help Yourself. I poured coffee into a Styrofoam cup and looked around: two guys were sitting at a table, the waitress was having a smoke. I asked how much, put sixty cents on the counter and took the coffee out to the car. It struck me then full-force that what I disliked in my own country was the lack of greeting between people, the indifference, even latent hostility. There was hardly ever a salutation coming or going, a civil exchange. At such moments I most missed living in Italy, where one entered a shop or bought a paper from a corner newsstand and was greeted, thanked, then said goodbye to. Here I am in the boondocks, I thought, and here it's different.

Yet the upstate country had a classical look. On the road to King Ferry I passed splendid large farmhouses with facades like Greek temples or with a kind of carpenter Gothic look. And they appeared to be rising up from fields of dried corn shucks. Very nice. At King Ferry I turned onto Route 90 and made the descent to Aurora on the lake. Then suddenly through the trees I saw the red brick Italianate tower of Main Building. I was there. Route 90 is Aurora's main street and overlooking it was the college splendidly situated on a hillside facing the lake. Over a bridged ravine is the junior residence, Glen Park, built in 1852 as the home of Henry Wells of Wells Fargo fame who left his fortune to found a college for women.

I rode into Aurora on a wave of euphoria, a feeling I had never had while attending college there. To be back in this remote countryside and see its beauty! To be back as an honored guest to give a workshop to students, dine at the President's home, and then do a reading after dinner. To be back to lay the ghost of the scared and unsteady girl of long ago who was known only for bananas in her room (always brought by my father, a wholesale fruit merchant, despite my humiliation and protests) and my watercolors of trees which came to be called by my name so peculiar to me were they. I had arrived a half hour before I was to meet the professor in the English department who had invited me. I parked at the post office and read on the board outside some historical notices about the founding of the village.

I walked up and down Main Street, noting the charm of the period houses, reveling even in being in such a bucolic backwater, enjoying the day. I was seeing what I never had in the past. Then the beauty and historicity had been lost on me because I was struggling to fit in, to have friends, to keep from being engulfed by girls who had had good educations while all I had had was an experience of rebellion at a convent school where I seemed to have been taught nothing. I could see how perfectly the backwater village fitted the Wasp girls who came from lines of mothers and grandmothers who had themselves been educated at Wells. Most of my classmates had the background and confident attitudes that could take in the charm; I was an outsider with the wrong kind of name engaged in desperate survival. Returning forty years later I saw Aurora for the first time as I walked Main Street. There was the Inn on the lake where I remember the fast, popular set of girls used to go to drink beer on Saturday evenings. Across from it was Wallcourt, the residence those same girls would choose after sophomore year, leaving the rest of us behind on campus. By junior year I had transferred to Syracuse University and lived at home. Yet how odd, I thought as I strolled, the classmates with whom I've kept up and whom I enjoy seeing wherever in the world they live, are those from Wells. And my most significant learning took place there.

I passed the small stone building that said BANK on its front; in a lovely yard I saw a huge oversize truck tire suspended from a tree as a swing. Across from the Inn was the Fargo Restaurant, and next to it a nice yellow house selling antiques in its own good time: hours were 12–5, Thursday to Saturday. And the Inn's shop opened only 12:30–3. There were historical markers along Main Street (were they there in my day?) and I learned what I had never known before: a General Sullivan had been there in September of 1779 to wipe out the Cayuga Indians in their settlement on the lake along with their orchards of 1,500 fruit trees. This same General Sullivan had devastated the Chemung Valley to the south near Elmira and destroyed the native peoples there, leaving in their remembrance only those odd town names I had passed on the way to Ithaca—Horseheads, Painted Post, Big Flats.

I looked for Miss Learned's little white cottage set on a rise above Main Street, remembering the occasions when she used to invite us, her freshman Spanish class, to have hot chocolate in the Castillian way, with olive oil floating on top. I have never forgotten that evil brew and how I had to get it down without gagging by thinking of the Christian martyrs; nor could I forget the thick lisp of her Castillian Spanish which she had us emulate rather than the more euphonious South American pronunciation. *Pobrecita,* she had long since passed away. And gone, too, were any other teachers of mine: Miss Bohannan who wanted me to stay and major in history with her; Miss Grether, my Latin professor, who gave me Catullus and the urge to go to Italy; Mr. Rideout of freshman composition class through which I struggled with a D+. I could no more write during those years at Wells than make the basketball team (though I had been captain of a winning team in high school as well as editor of the paper). I could not think, study, or do anything except pine for home. Since Syracuse was the main hub for those traveling to out-of-the-way Aurora during breaks, I would invite the Tibbies and Parkies and Smithies of my class (whose poise awed me and whom I longed to have as friends) to our new house on James Street. Word of my mother's great cooking got passed around so they always came.

Just after noon I returned to the Inn to meet the English professor and the library director for lunch. It was enjoyable. We spoke of environmental issues, President Bush's profound betrayal of Alaska as he aligned himself with Exxon, and his administration's general breeziness. I felt so equal! The professor had finally read my introduction to my collection of Italian American women writers called *The Dream Book* and pronounced it a superb and eloquent statement—something that should be reprinted in anthologies. It was a laying of old ghosts.

Confidence carried me into his classroom, since I had spent time on the student compositions he had sent me in advance and was prepared to discuss them (none of them very striking except for the one that started, "I met her at a baptism," and went on to describe, in fact, a baptism of fire by rape). But he had changed his plan and asked me to speak of myself as a writer. This strangely disconcerted me and I rambled. Did I present myself too modestly? Pass off the writing as too much for granted rather than the supreme effort it was? Belie my role in American literature as a voice for the submerged? I began to feel I was not effective. I began to recede into that long-ago student who was flunking freshman composition.

There was a break before the second part of the class. In that interval, we adjourned to the upstairs lounge in MacMillan where, I told the professor, I remembered Katherine Anne Porter sitting and chatting with a group of us after her reading. He moved off and I was left with a girl who said she was going to Florence her junior year and asked what it was like. I stuttered something.

The second part of the class was taken over by the professor and I began to feel ancillary, de trop. After class he headed me toward the new library, which he felt I should see, and he went home. I still hadn't any idea where to take my blouse still hanging in a protective garment bag in my car. I had been given directions to the professor's house after the library. He wanted me to meet his wife Bea, an art historian, who loved Italy, and to show me his lakeside dock. I had brought him a bottle of Bardolino and thought perhaps we would have a drink. Instead, he let me view his wife's attic domain—a wonderful space fitted with bookshelves, her writing desk, architectural windows. Then we stood on his dock while he told me of how Bea had been done out of tenure at a nearby university. He introduced his young daughter who was dressed, most engagingly, in a Halloween spider outfit concocted by Bea ("Bea can do anything!"). But by five o'clock I was tired and wanted someplace to rest and to change my clothes. Did he mean for me to change at his place? I finally asked him where I could hang my blouse.

He seemed to come to and said, Oh, of course, he would take me to my quarters in Main Building. I was given the Prophet's Chamber in Main, a place of remote and mysterious renown when I was a freshman at Wells. I tried to remember how it had gotten its name and its particular mystique but couldn't. I tried to meditate and couldn't. I decided to dress.

But the blouse, selected with such a sense of rightness, immediately looked glaringly, appallingly inappropriate. Once on I recognized how bare and exposed the loose cut left my unadorned neckline. The smart sleeves, slit to show a well-rounded, youthful arm, showed only the flab of aging flesh. I looked in the full-length mirror (the only amenity of the meager Prophet's Chamber) and was appalled: my arms and neck were not the youthful arms and neck of my mother, age twenty-three, in Paris. What a freak I seemed! How could I give witty, introductory blouse re-marks looking so weird? I would have to wear the suit I had driven up in and hide the blouse under the jacket. That still left my neck exposed and I regretted not having with me the Italian silk scarf my daughter Niki had given me for my birthday and which matched the autumn foliage. I could have swathed myself in it. I began to feel myself out of place and gauche.

I proceeded to dinner with the professor and his wife who was interesting—a kind of blowsy pre-Raffaelite character, her hair in an old-fashioned knob wisping out in strands. She had no discern-ible figure but was clothed in dark wrappings, loose top and shawl jacket over long skirt. Was she fat, thin? Who could tell? I was introduced around and met the president, an attractive, poised and personable young woman who had just given birth to her third child and was about the age of my youngest daughter. She was affable, friendly and excused herself during drinks to nurse her baby. That, at last, seemed progress. I felt glad for my old school where men and stuffy traditions had always ruled the roost. I was becoming restored to confidence.

I met the "Emily Dickinson person" of the English department and told her I was using the lines of Emily's "Our lives are so Swiss . . . but the other side stands Italy. . . ." as the theme of my new project. She raised her eyebrows in an unspoken question and moved on.

From dinner we proceeded to the MacMillan Lounge for my reading. A few people were already there, and I found out later they were mostly not from the college community which had the choice that same night of attending a play or Junior Blast. To fill the audience, the professor's mother, wife, and daughter had been dragooned into attendance. Very few—two or three—of his stu-dents were there. I spotted the librarian with whom we had lunched, thank God, and the Emily Dickinson person.

A woman blocked my way toward the lectern and said, "Do you know me?" I never know the answer to a question like that. I wondered if it could be the person from Ithaca who the professor told me wanted to meet me and have me sign one of my books. But no!—it was a former classmate of mine! Surprised and genuinely moved that she should have driven over from Geneva on the other side of the lake, I warmly embraced her. "You've lost weight," she said. She was remembering me when I was unhappy and weighed 150 pounds, when I would buy gallons of ice cream and hot fudge syrup from the sweetshop and stuff myself. When I went off by myself and sketched my idiosyncratic trees feeling alone and out of place.

After the reading, some in the audience told me they had read other of my work and I was glad. But I wondered how my evening's reading from an unpublished manuscript had gone; had it fallen on deaf ears? A student from the class I had met with earlier came up and addressed me by my first name saying she had met a former classmate of mine who had become an eminent archeologist in Guatemala and married there. When she described the person, I remembered a pale, pimply, shy girl who had seemed, if anything, even worse off than I.

The student went on to say she enjoyed my reading—I might have been describing her, she said, in the dialogue between a mother and daughter in a kitchen; she, too, had been anorexic. I was glad of the identification. And also by another thoughtful, pretty young woman who agreed about the eating theme, and who, the professor later said, was a wonderful poet and one of his best students ever. I signed four books. As everyone dispersed, my former classmate gave me the best words of the evening: "You were great—so poised and gracious." No one, it seemed had noticed the blouse, and I had forgotten about it.

The professor would have liked the evening to go on at his home with nightcaps, but his mother reminded him, "Bea's been teaching all day," and I, too, demurred. I was dropped off at the Prophet's Chamber. Removing the blouse, I vaguely wondered whether I had betrayed it or had myself been betrayed by it. In any case, I thought, I had come back to my old college; no further comebacks were needed. Some wisdom had accrued after all.

Driving back downstate, I heard over the radio of the death of Mary McCarthy the writer whom I had so admired, so wanted to be. Then at home I read in *The New York Times* the obituary of Dean Alfange, age 91, my mother's old suitor. He had been prominent; he had run for governor but she had not wanted to be his wife. Lack of nerve, she told me once. She, too, had failed in confidence in herself. I was, after all, my mother's daughter. Yet somehow we had both found our places in the world.

A Story of Rings

One March I was in Arizona—vast stretches of desert, ringed by strange, contorted mountains that look thrust out of the earth by volcanic forces as, indeed, they were.

Many years before, on a summer college program, I had had my first experience of Mexico and of seeing among its arts some stunning turquoise and silver jewelry; in Arizona I was seeing the jewelry again—this time of Navajo, Hopi, and contemporary American artisan origin. And I learned how turquoise is mined, extracted from a copper matrix in the Mule Mountains near Bisbee; how high-grade turquoise has an orangey bronze speckle flecking it and that an all-turquoise-color stone is likely just a powder residue of stones that have been ground to shavings and put together in a paste to form lower-grade turquoise stones.

Then there is the famed Bisbee Blue that is a patented trademark intended to increase market value and which is distinguished by dark speckles in its intense blue body. But the former geology professor who had defected from academia to run a stone shop in Brewery Gulch rather absent-mindedly let slip that the most precious quality of all is Persian turquoise and Arizona stones are next in line.

I looked at my own ring: three little turquoise ovals of different hues—one light turquoise with dark veins, the second a darker shade, and the third stone, green with no blue, but a crack. Turquoise, in fact, is a soft stone, subject to chipping if knocked around as my ring has been for the past many decades. And yet I find it handsome still, the stones set in a wide silver band separated by little silver spheres that embellish it. It is not a store ring. I purchased the loose stones in Mexico when I was on that class trip led by our Spanish professor. In the heart of Mexico City near the popular Sanborn's restaurant I found a street craftsman who fashioned the silver band to hold my three turquoise stones. He made my ring and the whole thing, stones and setting, cost around $10.00.

I called it my writer's ring, a visible sign of my promise to myself that I would be a writer. It was my first vow, before my marriage vow, and I wore the ring on the middle finger of my left hand. My ring has often been admired and I myself glance at it often. It is modest, but also elegant and eloquent. It spoke to me long ago of travel, exploration, new experiences, and of putting what mattered into words.

Once at a department store where I made a purchase the salesperson (teased hair, maroon fingernails, gum-snapping) had noted it when I was handing her payment and said, "Oh, I love that ring!"

Unwilling to engage her in conversation, I said a quick "thanks," and dropped my hand to my side.

But she had continued, "I'm into that Indian stuff, too— turquoise and silver."

For me it was not Indian stuff, nor even turquoise and silver stuff, but something much harder. It was pledging myself to an ideal, becoming a person in my own right, not just the lesser female part of a family or of an ethnic identity. It was not being that department store clerk; not being a stereotype.

After college I traveled. In Italy I met Antonio Barolini, a poet and journalist, with whom at first I could not speak, but listened entranced as he read his poetry to me. My Spanish dissolved into Italian and when he proposed, I accepted. The engagement ring he gave me is a beautiful chased white gold band on yellow gold set with a small diamond between two emeralds and was created by the famed Buccialatti jewelers. This ring, together with the traditional gold wedding band replaced the turquoise ring which remained put away during our married years as Antonio's work moved us between Italy and the United States. I ran our household, raised our family of three daughters, translated Antonio's stories of his Italian boyhood that appeared in *The New Yorker*, got a master's degree and had several part-time library jobs. At Antonio's sudden death in Rome, my wedding band went into the coffin with him, the poet who had been my partner and inspiration for twenty years. I returned to the United States and at some point put my writer's ring back on my middle finger. Recently I started wearing the Buccialatti ring next to it and find they do not clash, as I once thought my separate vows would.

Back in the States I paid my fee to attend a writers conference at the New School in New York City announced as "A Day with the Professionals"—and there, indeed, they all were: notable authors, editors, publishers. George Plimpton told a story of his once carrying on an interview with Ernest Hemingway in Venice as they walked along the Fondamenta. Hemingway was in his prime then, jovial and accessible, and George related how he took a chance and asked why, frequently, in Hemingway's work, a bird takes off during a lovemaking scene. Hemingway's eyes narrowed in rage, and, bent over George who was precariously at canal edge, he growled in fury, "Could you do better?" "No, Sir," said George managing to keep his footing. The audience laughed and I, fresh from Italy, recognized the double entendre of the bird and lovemaking that Hemingway must have picked up from his days as a young soldier in Italy during World War II. It was a good story and made me feel a part of things.

And I still recall from that conference the energizing thrill of hearing Cynthia Ozick speak of her own beginnings and how she grew. Soon after, I applied for and got a grant from the National

Endowment for the Arts which gave me the possibility to work on my first book, a generational novel called *Umbertina*. Naively, when it was published, I expected that it would be reviewed in *The New York Times* and be received as, finally, a story of the Italian American experience not based on the stereotypical mobs and mafia but, rather, the creative cross-cultural narrative it was, connecting Italy and America and told for the first time through the voices of the women who lived it. My book was not reviewed in *The New York Times*. I discovered that I had no mainstream connections, no advocates, no reviewers. I awoke to the reality of how different it was for me to be an author from what it had been for Antonio Barolini.

A leather-framed photo from Antonio's desk that now sits on mine depicts perfectly the background for the confident air Italian writers like Antonio have: shown in the distance is a classic Paladian villa reflected in a long waterway that comes to the foreground where a small band of geese gather at water's edge. In the photo, above the villa, someone had penned in *"l'arte;"* alongside the honking geese was written *"la critica."* Antonio and his cronies could well mock the honks and jeers of critics or reviewers, so assured were they of their own place as writers. Not I. As an exemplar of a quite unfamiliar voice in the national literature, I needed an interpreter beyond either classic permanence or critical honks.

I did not fit into the context of my national literature as Antonio so deftly did his. I am not the writer my Italian husband was. Not that he was "better" (he may well have been, though such comparisons are odious and beside the point), but that he was confident of his belonging. He was supremely at ease with the fact of his calling as a writer, confident of being a literary person without having to question his right to be, or whether he was odd to be. Literature was his unquestioned patrimony and privilege; and when he practiced it, he was automatically in the club.

I was left with questions: how do Italian American women become writers out of the negating signals of their lives? How do they use their individual selves narratively to oppose and/or understand the Otherness of the dominant society? Who, in fact, are they and why are they not known? What I was to find was that we write ourselves to know ourselves; we write of our differences in order to embrace them. I explored this in the introduction to *The Dream Book*, a kind of *apologia pro vita mea*. My Italian husband didn't need such a statement; he simply wrote out of who he was and for the literature of which he was a part.

He well knew who his family was and what their position in their community had always been. And if he had questions, he could read their letters, ledgers, school books, diaries, etc., or look for them in the family albums or, indeed, in the histories of his region. On his father's side, they had been Venetian sea captains for centuries; on his mother's side, they were the slightly zany landed gentry of the Veneto, all providing material for those delightful stories of his which appeared in my English translation in *The New Yorker* for a number of years. But when I wrote my own stories, my past and the characters from it were not, in the words of a *New Yorker* editor, "the right material" for them. An Italian childhood had the right cachet—Italian American was something else.

I do not define myself as an Italian American writer. To be a writer is enough. And I believe what Gabriel Garcia Marquez has said: "The duty of a writer, the revolutionary duty if you like, is simply to write well." And yet, as Isaac Bashevis Singer has also said, when he looks in the mirror in the morning, who looks back at him is a man of Polish Jewish origin in whose skin he lives and writes. And so I, too, live in my Americanized, Italianate, female skin and write from it. And crucial to the matter of how I perceive myself is how others do. And my name colors that perception.

I was not alone. I found this out from compiling writings by women of my background and creating an anthology, *The Dream Book*. But the times were changing, various voices were coming into our national literature. When I was invited to contribute an essay to a literary review's special issue on ethnicity and literature I wrote "Becoming a Literary Person out of Context," my hard-won understanding of the situation for writers like me, the so-called "women of the shadows" (an insidious phrase taken out of the context of Ann Cornelisen's book about past peasant culture in Southern Italy and misapplied to Italian American women). Quite simply, we were not expected to be writers! Much less write about ourselves.

I considered Medea. She, the barbarian princess, the foreigner, was the ultimate outsider to culturally correct Jason, the Greek insider. And her rage against him was also at his contempt for her being "other." It is what informs the writing of all those who are perceived as different.

But let me return to Arizona. For being there brought to mind, along with my terrestial turquoise ring, the celestial rings of Saturn that Carolyn Porco, then a professor at the University of Arizona, was at that very time studying. I was visiting my cousin Bob outside Tucson and tried to call Carolyn but got only an answering machine and no return call to my message.

At his retirement Bob and his wife Jan had fled the climate of the Northeast for that of the Southwest. They have a hacienda style home set off by various cacti in the front and a spacious patio overlooking a pool in the back. Hummingbirds hover around feeders, the view is to the distant mountains that frame Tucson, and there is desert calm and small animals all around. Bob and Jan collect beautiful art works—the weavings of the Navajo, Hopi bowls, and the sculpture of an important local artist. Their home itself, low and softly hued, is an artful work set into the land around it. Jan gave me a showing of her beautiful native jewelry—

belts set with coral and turquoise, pins, pendants, heavy silver bracelets embossed with Indian motifs, necklaces, earrings. She has a uniquely beautiful squash blossom necklace—not the usual heavy piece so prominently displayed in stores in town, but a chain of delicate blossoms exquisitely light and elegant with silver and turquoise blendings. Her jewelry is rich and valuable, and beside it my writer's ring is indeed the poor cousin. But no one thinks to make a comparison, and in this case what would be the point? On my visit I have brought them copies of my most recent books, the pledge of my writer's ring fulfilled.

For by the time I got there Arizona itself subtly echoed the subject of much of my writing—the vexed question of identity. On a day-trip to Nogales, on the border with Mexico, we came upon a crowd listening to the local high school's student mariachi band. Their leader was an ex-Big Band trumpet player who had been at the Julliard School and then found his way west to that little border town where most of the population is called Mexican American. In fact, the students who played and sang in Spanish for us, so comely and poised and talented, were of all hues and facial types though some of the spectators wondered aloud if they were Mexican or American. It seemed clear to me that since they lived in Nogales, Arizona and were students at the local high school, they were indeed American. But people were calling them Mexican American. Just as I have been called an Italian American. Why are we not, finally, just American? Because our names are not Anglo? For that is the great divide in Arizona—Mexicans, Indians, and Anglos. Anyone not dark-eyed and dark-complexioned is Anglo.

If Arizona gave me back the identity problem, it also gave me the stars. Where I live in a Hudson River village there is a great deal of light pollution in the night sky from nearby New York City. We never get the deep, dark canopy of a desert sky with its thick sprawl of sparkling stars, constellations, planets. My cousin Bob, of course, has a telescope and though the time we used it the sky was too much lit by a gleaming gibbous moon to be an optimum star-gazing night, still there was Orion's belt as clear as anything, and a Big Dipper that looked so close I might reach up and tip it. But it was not a night to focus on stars or planets, so we spied the moon—its seas and craters and the strange fringes on its edge that looked like pieces of crust about to drop off.

And I thought of far places, of time's passage, of the long journey to realize the promise of my writer's ring even though at most it might only admit me to George Garrett's anthology of overlooked and now forgotten writers. And I thought of Carolyn Porco, brought up in the Bronx the daughter of Italian immigrants, now become a top planetary scientist, whom I had first met years before through her brother Peter. She had studied the stars and was herself a star—the designated "ringleader" of the Imaging Team for the Cassini mission to explore Saturn and its rings.

Carolyn's brother Peter was editor-in-chief of a local magazine for which I had been writing when he invited me to a family party in Connecticut one summer day. That's where I first met her—stunning, tall, slim, her oval face framed by a mop of magnificent dark curly Italian hair. She herself was in constant touch with her hair, lifting up strands, twining it around a finger, patting it or pulling it severly back from her face. She wore sweatpants and running shoes as did Roger, her boyfriend of that time, to whom she gave exaggerated attention, I thought, he being opinionated and unpleasant. Carolyn and Roger kissed and fondled at the table obviously to taunt and outrage her father who sat apart and sullenly watched his daughter.

Peter was proud of his sister's achievements and had often spoken about her. It made me think that Carolyn and I had things in common—each of us having been the only girl in a family of boys, each of us having had a partial Catholic-school education meant to mold us into a handmaiden role in life regardless of our ambitions. I could still hear the mocking tone of Sister Matilda who liked to taunt me as she'd point to me in her history class and say, "Let's hear from our shining star about the Congress of Vienna." But my motto came from Sister Aquiline's Latin class: *nil desperandum.*

Carolyn and I even shared the fine-tuning of our names, for I had in college and for some time afterward made my name Helyn; and she was Carolyn, not, as she stressed to reporters, to be called Caroline in their stories. Peter later told me that she was baptized Clara, the Americanized version of their mother's name Chiara; and as a child she was nicknamed Princess and called Prinny or Principessa, but she hated all those names and, growing up and wanting to be distinctly separated from her mother's naming and from any of the family's non-American peculiarities, she changed herself to Carolyn.

I engaged Carolyn in conversation, congratulated her on her work and compared her discoveries on the edge of the solar system to the discoveries of Columbus, Magellan. Smiling at me disarmingly she said, "You're not the first to have said that." And besides, she noted, as a scientist she was interested in pursuing the truth, not the applications (often improper) that countries and governments make of scientific discoveries as was done, for example, in exploitation of the New World following Columbus's voyages.

Who could disagree with her?

Some family history came out that day—how Carolyn had grown up seeing her mother under her father's thumb, a position she vowed never to be in. She never asked him to finance her education. She earned her own way starting in high school by working in libraries, then in a shoe store and as a secretary. Her father balked at her desire to go to college, saying girls should get married; an expensive education was wasted on them. When she studied astronomy, he said, "Where will that get you?" By the time she was in graduate school she had a stipend and had separated herself from the legacy of her mother's docility and what she saw as the family style. But even as she changed her baptismal name, from some paradoxical sense of pride or perhaps simply Calabrian hard-headness, she kept the family surname.

Carolyn's recollections of early intense religious experiences as she tried to be rigorously Catholic and observant, reminded me of my own youthful infatuation with the Church and its rituals. Then she was drawn to Eastern religions and philosophy and finally the Cosmos called her by way of astronomy. Today her final position is what I can take for mine: there are cosmic energies and forces, but the universe itself is not focused on us, our strivings good or bad. What we search for is patterns, whether through science or religion; and a pseudoscience like astrology is just an example of the human need to make patterns and something predictable out of the unknown. There are no creationists among scientists, Carolyn said. And even in her observant Catholic days, she said, she always thought of the creation story as mythology or metaphor. I told her that was smart of her: being brought up in the Bronx, and so a New Yorker, she had more early savvy than would have been possible to a child like me in Syracuse.

Still I recognized in her childhood story what I had experienced a generation earlier: coming both from our family backgrounds and the general society's non-expectations for us, we were not thought to achieve anything other than a suitable marriage. Perhaps it was that non-expectation that goaded us. It was also that we were entranced—I with literature, she with the cosmos.

In my time an Italian American woman had to be self-birthed, without models, without inner validation, and without the outer world's expectation that she could or should succeed, and that what she creates will ever receive respectful attention or be valued. For me, growing up, an Italian American woman was a stranger both to literature and in literature. Inwardly besieged by doubts (for she is betraying her destiny of self-giving in the service of others), and tormented by the insinuation of hubris as she aspires to go beyond her cultural boundaries, if she does persist in the struggle to achieve, she must make a gigantic leap of faith and imagination.

As was the case for me and, though somewhat less a generation later, still a factor for Carolyn. To be a recognized writer I presumed that I would have to change my Italian surname just as, once, English and American singers had Italianized their names to enter the world of opera. I could do it myself or through an astute name-changing marriage. But I didn't marry for nomenclature; I went from one Italian surname to another.

Carolyn changed only her given name to show that she was self-made into a new person.

And it hadn't been easy. She was timid when she first got to graduate school at the California Institute of Technology, chosen because its ties with the Jet Propulsion Lab would help get her involved in space exploration. And that hunch proved to be right. But she had quickly to acquire a very positive sense of self-esteem in order to survive in that highly competetive male environment. She is also intuitive—a female advantage?—and that has given her the ability to arrive at insights missed by others.

She is determined and tough-minded but also aggrieved that she is known as a "pushy bitch" whereas a man in her place would be admired as an achiever. She still sees discrepancies in gender behavior and perceptions all around her, not only in her old-time family. Reporters have turned vengeful when she hasn't been able to give them the time they demand. One who wrote about her was totally unfair, she said, characterizing her as a tough bully who shouted and slammed the phone on him, which was quite untrue.

"Rings are her things," an early newspaper story about Carolyn had as its lead sentence. I was fifty-four when my first book was published; Carolyn was much younger when in 1989, as leader of the Voyager 2 team for its Neptune flyby she stood before a throng of reporters from around the world to describe five newly discovered rings circling the huge blue planet Neptune. The reportage on Carolyn describes her as one of the leading experts on planetary rings and the accompanying photo shows her beautiful, poised, confident, and still framed by that luxuriant mop of dark, curling hair.

There was a touching note to our conversation when she asked me if I minded being alone. Was she, I wondered to myself, asking herself that question? I've had a family, I told her, I did it the old-fashioned way, family first. I've been a late starter and I'll never know how it might have been otherwise. And I wondered about her disconnect from family.

"Do you live alone?" I asked.

"Yes!" She exclaimed, smiling broadly, "There are absolutely no high-maintenance items in my life—no plants, pets, or husbands."

But there had been serious relationships, Peter said, and still lots of Beatles memorabilia—as a girl she used to think one day of having four boys and naming them John, Paul, George, and Ringo.

I tell her she is a magnificent role model for all women, but especially for Italian American women and she is glad. Then I told her my own stunned reaction when my then next-door neighbor asked me, accusingly, why I always wrote about Italians. She was a Wasp married to a Jew who had never asked herself why John Cheever always wrote about suburban Wasps or Saul Bellow about alienated Jews. Were they, to her, Americans while the Italian Americans in my fiction were not? Why had she used the term "Italians" for them? I was writing about people as American as any of the characters in Cheever or Bellow. And so my answer to her was, "I don't write about Italians, I'm writing about Americans." What I didn't add was that the Americans I wrote about were particularly alienated because of people like her who created Outsiders and Insiders in a shared culture.

Many years later I heard the African author Chinua Achebe address an audience on his life as a writer. Once, in Australia, he said, he was asked by a young woman at his lecture if he were always going to write about Africans, or if he had a plan to write about people in general. Taken aback for a few seconds, he swiftly realized that what she meant by "people in general" were white Anglo-descended people like her, not people like him. He then answered, No. Of course. What Achebe so masterfully wrote of was the human condition, not just "people like him." What my neighbor was used to reading was "people like her"—not the so-called "Italians" I was writing about.

All this came to mind when I was invited to speak at a conference at the University of Bordeaux titled "Interculturalism and the Writing of Difference." What an elegant way to put it, I thought—not ethnic writing, or marginal, or even multicultural, but the writing of difference—*Écrire la différence*—*et vive la différence!*

Years have passed since my meeting with Carolyn in Connecticut—I did not connect with her in Arizona and then learned from Peter she had moved on to the Space Science Institute in Boulder, Colorado. I keep my clippings about her—*The New Yorker*'s "Annals of Space" piece, the notice of her lecturing at the 92nd Street Y on "The World Beyond," the writeup about her appearance on a panel discussing the role of female scientists in film or TV portrayals where she is quoted as saying that the real drama is in the confrontation of ideas and the quest for truth, which is what science is all about.

In July 2004, Dr. Carolyn Porco reported on the Cassini's spacecraft photos of Saturn's giant moon, Titan. She was photographed in front of a giant close-up and quoted as saying the results of the mission were not as clear as they had hoped. Her hair is short now; she looks older and wears glasses. But she still has her exuberant hopes and finds her career mind-blowing. Indeed, she has her celestial rings—rings that were believed to circle only Saturn have now been shown around three other planets as well.

I consider her a heroine of our times, not only because of the difficulties she had to overcome in her early family life, but also those she encountered in her career. Her work has been her life; she has never reconciled with her father, and keeps in touch only sporadically with her brothers, and has not gotten back to me when I've written her my congratulations on her newest achievements. I guess, in Peter's words, she is truly out of this world. And I think that is both grand, and achieved at great price. But only she knows that being starstruck was worth it.

The struggle to become the persons we want to be—beyond the context of birth and the world's non-expectations—is only some of the story. In Arizona I fitted together the more personal story of rings and aspirations: my writer's ring for me and Carolyn's cosmic ones for her.

A Circular Journey

The place names in my personal lexicon—where I was born, where my family came from, and where I have lived and studied—are classical: Syracuse, Croton, Utica, Magna Graecia, Rome, Aurora. They are in America, or they are in Italy; some are in both places.

My hometown was Syracuse but at the time I was growing up the name gave off no Old World, classical ring to me; it was a hard-nosed upstate New York locale committed to commercial interests. It was a place not much given to "culture," where opera or ballet, when they came by, had to be seen in the auditorium at Central High School. It's the place where, despite Syracuse University's hosting the state College of Forestry, the lofty elms that canopied James Street with deep shade are gone, dead of Dutch elm disease. Even the weather is ungenerous in Syracuse; I remember heavy, humid summers that lay on one like a thick shawl of rags, and long miserable winters with just enough nice days in between to show us what we were missing elsewhere. No one ever comes to Syracuse to vacation.

Syracuse sounded ominously like "circuitous" to me, setting up images of a ferret on a Ferris wheel circling always in the same direction, getting nowhere. And it was its heaviest the summer I graduated from the Convent School and was waiting to enter my freshman year at Wells College. It was a strange, fitful summer filled with longings to be free from the old while apprehensive and unsure of the new; I was in limbo, neither saved nor lost, just waiting.

We spent summers on Oneida Lake, a steely grey body of water fourteen miles or so out of town, where my parents played golf at the old Syracuse Yacht and Country Club at South Bay. I swam in the lake and for years imagined myself swimming to Frenchman's Island which had a lighthouse and lay about a mile and half away. The Yacht Club was boring to me and only the island and my idea of getting there held any interest for I felt different from the golfers, the going-steady couples of my high school friends, even my family.

It was that summer while I waited to be out of Syracuse and other encirclements that I went downtown and purchased my first book of poetry, T. S. Eliot's *Four Quartets*. It was the sign of something, but I hardly knew what. I bought the book at Emily Mundy's bookshop on Warren Street across from the original Schrafft's restaurant. Certainly the nuns hadn't ever spoken of T. S. Eliot. No poets more recent or less Catholic than Alice Meynell or Francis Thompson ever reached our ears. So how was I drawn to Eliot? (Elective affinities, my future husband would later remark wryly.) Perhaps I had read in *Life* magazine that Eliot was the eminence of our times, and there learned of "The Wasteland," whose title alone would have drawn me to him. In any case, though my best friends, Kathleen and Camille, thought it weird of me, I continued to carry Eliot around with me all summer at the Yacht Club even to the dock where we sunbathed and looked across the lake to the thick green clump of trees that was Frenchman's Island and where we made our plans for the big swim.

They were lazy, nonurgent plans: we would need someone to follow with a boat; we would have to train, swimming farther and farther from the dock each time; we should set a target date when there was less chance that one of those sudden storms the sullen lake was so famous for would come up. But the plans were desultory—neither Kathleen nor Camille took the swim as seriously as I did, for they both had boyfriends that summer and I was the extra on the fringe of their foursome, feeling odd and out of place.

I wasn't popular with boys, my mother said, because I always had my nose in a book. Popular? Who cared about popular, I scoffed. I would meet and marry a poet . . . I would be a poet. And that, unknown, was the real goal of that summer, more than Frenchman's Island.

In the fall I would be gone, and not to a to a saints-name college the others chose, but to Wells, a college honoring an enterprising businessman, Henry Wells of Wells Fargo fame and fortune who had believed in educating women.

Before we parted in late summer, Kathleen, Camille, and I did get to Frenchman's Island—not by swimming but by borrowing an outboard from Camille's boyfriend. The growth was very thick on the island and we didn't go near the lighthouse which was in the keep of Mr. Hinterwalder who also had the fish fry place and roller skating pavilion at South Bay. We stayed near the shore, having a picnic and taking pictures of ourselves. I remember how lonely and wild the island seemed, how far from the skaters and music of South Bay. It seemed marooned, a patch of underbrush and trees in the middle of the dreary grey lake. Like its neighbor, Dunham's Island, its wild remoteness had been the main thing about it. Or so it seemed to me then.

When I did get away, it wasn't just to Aurora, New York, where Wells is located, but to places well beyond, by way of Latin seminar. I had taken years of high school Latin without being fully awakened to its robust beauty; that came when, with only two other students, I was in Miss Grether's seminar on the Latin elegiac poets. Through Tibullus, Catullus, Propertius, and Ovid—but especially Catullus—there surfaced in me unsuspected and deep longings for the classical Mediterranean world, and for an Italy from which, after all, I had my descent but which heretofore was present in my life only as an embarrassment.

My name now became a link with the classical world that I was discovering as superb and stirring. I knew nothing of my Italian background except that my grandparents had all come from Italy. Neither the gourmet age nor that of ethnic pride had yet dawned in America; it was still melting-pot time, the time of getting ahead by homogenizing into what everyone else thought we should be.

In my family, but not in the families of my friends, there was an old woman in black, my grandmother Nicoletta, who didn't speak English and had strange, un-American ways of dressing and wearing her hair; even what she grew in the backyard garden was odd, not American—no one then knew zucchini, broccoli rabe, or basil. No matter the distance, Italy, the enemy of our country in World War II, cast dark shadows over us. How could we ignore the relationship which our name made clear? And in the pain were many confusions: must we hate Italy because of fascism? For there was also pride in the Italy of the great names in art and music. But then hadn't that same Italy spewed out millions of its poor people, relieved to see them go off as emigrants? Italian Americans seemed estranged from Italy, and not much cared for in America, either.

It all hurt. Everything hurt in those days—not being popular, being bookish, being Italian, losing the faith. And at the college freshman banquet where prophetic place-cards marked one, mine read "Someday I shall find my place in the world," marking me, I was sure, less an adventurer than an insecure dolt. Then the Roman elegiac poets came like shafts of serene, civilized light into my personal murk. Catullus was my education, and he led me straight to Italy, to which my life became joined, for in meeting Italy I also met the poet whom I married. And there I, too, wrote poetry. My going to Italy was, at first, upsetting to my parents, who felt that in marrying an Italian I had regressed in contrast to my brothers who married Anglo or Irish Americans. But as with the Latin poets, Antonio Barolini the poet from Vicenza, had brought light into my life and I didn't doubt that marrying him was the right, the fated thing to do.

We were married in Vicenza, not far from Sirmione on Lake Garda where can be found the olive groves and Roman ruins known as the site of Catullus's villa. *"Salue, o venusta Sirmio. . . ."* Catullus wrote in the poem which spoke his joy at seeing it again; and my joy at seeing that lake—so blue after the grey of Oneida and so humanized with villas and terraced hillsides after the lake cottages and fast-food stands of South Bay, was just as intense. Even before I knew Italian well, Antonio had wooed me reading aloud his ode to Catullus, and the first Italian I memorized were his own lines from that poem:

> *ora la fanciulla è sogno,*
> *sogno il poeta e l'amore.*

We went to Sicily on our honeymoon and saw the original Syracuse; and just over the sea in Tunisia, twenty miles from the ruins of Carthage, excavations were going on at the ancient Utica that had given its name to the upstate city near Syracuse where my mother's immigrant parents settled. I was discovering the classical origins of place names that had signified nothing to me when, growing up, I lived among them in upstate New York.

There is nothing certain in life except *l'imprevidibile*, the unforeseen. No sooner were we settled in our Italian life than I found myself back in Syracuse when Antonio was appointed consul general there. In the tradition of consuls (Hawthorne in Liverpool, Stendahl at Civitavecchia), he proceeded to write a novel between his occasional duties of notarizing papers and deeds for the Italian Americans of Syracuse who still had dealings with Italy, or attending Columbus Day banquets.

Syracuse had always meant an uncomfortable knowledge of Italian background, it had meant poor and mistaken values. But now I realize that the trouble was not just Syracuse and myself and my friends and family there; it was an American circumstance of growing up when I did; it was the last vestige of isolationism and containment in the little American dream world where young people could drift about a yacht club summer after summer, having no greater demand on their minds than how to be popular or to swim to Frenchman's Island.

I no longer resist Syracuse in the old way, and though I haven't returned to live there, I have thought of being buried there. But how I arrived at that idea makes up the long and circular journey I am relating.

After Antonio's stint as consul in Syracuse, we returned with a new baby daughter to Italy where we did not live ever after but between our two countries—one golden interlude in Croton-on-Hudson and another in Rome. It was while we lived in Rome that I made the trip the summer of 1967 to Calabria, the Magna Graecia of antiquity, to see the village of Castagna where my grandmother, that old woman in black, and her husband Angelo had been born. *Castagna* is also the Italian word for chestnut and this had long ago given rise to my father's quip, "Castagna is where all the nuts come from." His own family had come from the environs of Messina in Sicily which he considered a superior provenance in that curious game indulged in by Italian Americans as to which unpreposing old-country birthplace was better or worse than another.

My parents had actually been to Castagna, the diminished last lap of a wedding trip that had started with Paris and Rome. Their mortifying experience of Castagna had taken place in a rainy late November and has become part of family folklore, much smoothed over by time into a now humorous story. They had gotten there by horse and buggy, up over lonely mountain roads where, as night came on, the driver, sinisterly named (it seemed to my mother) Malerba, had to get out to crack his whip in all directions in front of the horses to frighten away any wolves lurking in the deep forests. In the ancestral village they were greeted by torchlight and, in the mud and dark, led to a ladder up which my mother climbed in her Paris outfit to a windowless loft where they passed the night. In answer to my father's question about a toilet, a door had been flung open onto the dark night along with the unnerving answer, "Anywhere! Anywhere!" They fled the next morning without ever taking a look at where they had been.

Decades later I drove to Calabria with my third daughter Nicoletta, *detta* Niki, and my cousin Donna from Utica who was spending a Fulbright year in Italy as researcher in Renaissance music. Everyone thought we were mad to go to Calabria in August. The Calabrians I knew in Rome said, "Calabria isn't a place to go to, it's a place to leave," for intellectual Calabrians have a furtive feeling about their land. They cannot talk about it except in a sad, disparaging, outraged way. They still feel the complexes of the benighted region which couldn't keep them, and yet, because they've left, they feel guilty as well. This differentiates them from those poor Calabrians like my grandparents who, once they had left, did not look backward in guilt, but only ahead in relief. My grandparents felt grateful for the rest of their lives in getting safely to America where they could give their children a future rather than the burdens of the past.

And yet . . . and yet, nothing is that simple, especially the ties and binds of one's beginnings. Where one grew up remains the backdrop of one's mind, the panorama against which everything else is played out. My grandmother Nicoletta had tended goats in the chestnut and oak forests of Calabria's mountainous interior and had drunk from the stream that ran to the valley below her village. When she left those scenes she left for good, for she was a strong woman, utterly directed to whatever sacrifice was necessary for the sake of the future. She made that one great trip in her lifetime and then stopped. She never spoke of Calabria, was satisfied to have come to the New World where her sons prospered, but when she lay dying in Utica her last words had asked for water from the mountain spring in the woods near Castagna. Or had she? Did I hear this from my mother or was I already creating the fictional character of my novel *Umbertina*?

I was never able to speak to my grandmother Nicoletta, for she spoke only a dialect, the sounds of which were harsh and grating to my ears, and I spoke only English in those days. Ever since learning Italian I have wished for a chance to go back in time to be able to speak to her; but would it have been communication?— she with her native south dialect and I with my acquired, Veneto-accented high language? She was silent in her Utica kitchen, yet transformed into Umbertina; when she lay dying, I have her remember the Castagna spring. She was the true model for Umbertina, but I had invented her.

She had raised her large family, helped advance their livelihoods from keeping a grocery store to establishing finally a large wholesale-food business; and yet she had remained content to tend her garden and to cook her soups over a big black range in the kitchen. I don't remember ever seeing her in the front parlors. She lived with her eldest son and his large family in a Queen Anne house of fishtail shingles with turrets and porches, sliding doors between parlors, and a grand oak stairway with a window seat in its landing bay; it was her final home (and the only one known to me)—the last visible sign of her progress. She did not attempt other ways or values than those with which she had been born and would die. She was honest and didn't expect her American children to be as she was; nor did she try to be what they were. She must always have known that the price of her uprooting would be to have alien children, and grandchildren with whom she could not speak. And yet the notion of keeping up was foreign to the woman who had moved her physical whereabouts in the world but not her inner locus.

I myself have moved more than a dozen times. Home is where you hang your hat, they say; mine is where I hang above my writing desk the little tin heart with its primitive hammered design and tapering sheath that my grandmother wore at her side to keep her knitting needles handy while she pastured her goats in Calabria and knit thick stockings for the coming winter. I am moved that the little tin heart accompanied her to the New World where she never expected to herd goats, and that, after her death, it turned up among her few personal possessions and was claimed by my mother who gave it to me, my totem.

However, when I set out for Calabria, it wasn't just for Castagna, the place where all the nuts came from, though it was that, too. It was also for Magna Graecia, a fabled place, the home of the Western Greeks, the place of some ancestry far more remote than my grandparents, and the site of the original Kroton which perhaps gave its name to the village on the Hudson where Antonio and I once lived and about which he wrote in the poetry collection called *Elegie di Croton*. All the place-names of my lexicon connected and directed me south to that land known as the *mezzogiorno*, midday, because the sun always seems at its noon zenith there.

Living in Rome had imparted a potent but impure clue to antiquity. It was the trip to the South that most revealed the classical message, beginning with Paestum and its splendid plain of temples. Then there was the Gulf of Palinuro below the promontory of the same name, a gulf named for Aeneas's helmsman who fell asleep at the wheel and dropped into the sea at that point and had his burial on the coast. I had read his sad tale in my old Convent School days when taking Vergil with Sister Aquiline, that pale and finely featured beauty whose cool disdain of the world beyond

Latin was the whole essence of her detached monastic bearing. One of Antonio's poems, in my translation from Italian, has these lines:

> And I, too, in drowsiness,
> closing my eyes,
> like Palinurus
> will fall from the ship's side
> into the iridescent wake:
> gentle sea,
> delicious folly
> love.

And I hadn't known until I got there that there was a geographic as well as an emotional place which evoked the Trojan.

Beyond the Gulf of Palinuro was Velia, the ancient Elea where the Eleatic school of philosophy flourished under Parmenides, a prototype existentialist; and then there was Maratea, the gem of the whole coast, between blue sea and golden, broom-covered mountainside. Just below Maratea we entered the region of Calabria, and at Paola we turned inland from the coast and crossed the mountains to Cosenza, where in antiquity Hannibal had passed in retreat and, later, Alaric the Visigoth arrived in triumph fresh from his sack of Rome in A.D. 410.

Once we descended the mountains we were in parched land, the disconsolate, stifling landscape which signifies Calabria; the word *brullo* kept coming to mind: bare, stripped, barren, bleak, desolate, scorched, the color of a crème brulée. I became uncertain faced with that ravaged landscape. It seemed that an indecent curiosity was propelling me in those August dog days seven hundred kilometers over mountains and hot plains to visit a village which I would simply look at and then leave, a tourist of my own provenance. Yet I knew I could not arrive in Calabria with the detachment of a George Gissing, say, or Norman Douglas, Edward Lear. They were exploring the country through the distant perspective of their old school education only, not seeking the very roots from which they grew. They could and did turn objective British eyes on Calabria, for they were not looking at themselves as I was.

I began to feel that going to Calabria would only confirm everyone's having left; would only confirm forever and again the purifying power of money and the lure of America which provided it. Money buys the soap that makes the difference between me, clean and presentable and educated, and them, the despised *meridionali*. Americans who travel to Italy have always understood this—they travel to the center and north, avoid the south.

It's evolution that put me on gorgeous, empty Calabrian beaches along the Ionian Sea to raise the Marie Antoinette-esque question, "Why don't these people swim at their own beaches?" Because, of course, they have to survive, not sun and swim, and because the Saracen incursions left them with a diffidence toward the sea from which the brutalities arrived. The coasts of Magna Graecia in decline had been no Côte d'Azur but a place of terror and pillage, slavery and worse.

Was there any point in my trying to connect Magna Graecia with my people of Castagna? I was going to a village of the interior at a remove, deliberately, from the glorious Hellenized cities of the coast. What was the indulgence of Sybaris, or the philosophizing on the cosmos by Pythagoras at Kroton, or the elegant epigrams of the woman poet Nossis in Locri to the inhabitants of mountain villages in the forests? Nothing, nothing. The indigenous people—the Bruttii, as the Romans called them—were an austere and reserved people, diffident not only to the culture of Greece but to all strangers. *Bruttii a brutis moribus*—Bruttians from their brute habits, Horace punned. And yet the overtones of Magna Graecia must have reached them, too; each racial invasion had washed against them—for how else would my grandfather have had his stature and the clear blue eyes that led him to be called *Il normanno*, the Norman, except for that intermingling of Northmen's blood with the women of the South? And it is certain that those of the North arrived in the fastness of the hills around Castagna: the remains of the eleventh-century Norman abbey I came upon in the valley below Castagna attest to that.

There are few monuments of antiquity or even of later ages in the region. What the internecine fighting of the early Greek cities didn't wipe out, earthquakes did. At Capo Colonna near modern Crotone, replacing ancient Kroton, the lone remaining column of what the ancients knew as a splendid temple of Hera Lakinia is a fitting symbol of ravaged Calabria.

I grew to detest those guidebooks that spoke rhetorically of the harsh beauty and severe charm of Calabria, completely covering up the dread fact that this is a region which was not originally and naturally harsh but had become so through greed and unconcern. Each invader felled the forests, and the last plunderers were the Calabrian barons who lived in Rome or Naples and never visited their lands but, when they needed money, simply gave orders to have more trees cut for market. The treeless soil loosened; the watersheds disappeared; the rivers clogged up with stones and bushy growth when the winter torrents subsided, the little pools that were left became the stagnant breeding places of malaria. Sickness and poverty became chronic. Those who could get away, did; those who were left were the hopeless sick—those whom the northerners scorned as indolent.

Corrado Alvaro, the Calabrian author of *Revolt in Aspromonte*, has spoken of the centuries-long solitude of Calabria. And he has said that, despite the various ethnic components of that region, whoever has an experienced eye, a Calabrian eye, can always distinguish a countryman, no matter what his surroundings, by his air of reserve, diffidence, reflectiveness; by the naturalness which marks all his acts and by the inbred, despairing view of life that his demeanor bespeaks. The Milanese is an entrepreneur, the Roman a bureaucrat, and the Calabrian a philosopher.

Between instep and toe of the Italian boot, Castagna is in that lovely forested part of Calabria known as the Sila (from the Latin *silva* for forest)—and, more precisely, as the Sila Piccola—to differentiate it from the Sila Greca and the Sila Grande which lie north and east. It's about a two-hour drive from Cosenza on a twisty mountain road that was almost bare of traffic. Once in a while we would see a pack peddler on a motorcycle, from both sides of which were slung gaudy plastic wares and jugs so that vehicle and load caricatured a donkey bearing amphorae on his sides; or there'd be a woman walking toward the nearest hamlet with a basket of brilliant zucchini blossoms on her head; or a boy sitting rakishly backwards on his mount, waving as we passed.

Here, at last, were forests and some fertile valleys, though the rivers which Cicero had described as "noble" and navigable (not to mention harbors—"See the harbors of Velia," says Vergil in the sixth book of the *Aeneid*), were modest summer streams. There had been Greek overland trade routes through this region which some historians claim still retains its Greek spirit today. But not so, counters Norman Douglas in *Old Calabria*: in the uplands of the Sila, the Bruttian spirit has dominated as evidenced by the comportment of the women. These are not the supine types of the coast, where the Ionic influence resulted in a depreciation of the female, as happens, Douglas said, wherever Greek and Saracen strains are to be found; the Bruttian-descended women of the mountains are handsome, intelligent, healthy women who are treated quite differently from those of the lowlands.

But many, many racial strains fed the mainstream of people here. Along with Greeks, there were Lucanians, Romans, the North Africans with Hannibal, Byzantines and Saracens, Normans, Lombards, Swabians from the Black Forest, Spanish Bourbons, Napoleonic French, and Hapsburgs. There have also been eccentric English visitors like Crauford Ramage, George Gissing, Norman Douglas, and Edward Lear on their walking trips, and, finally, Italian Americans in floral drip-dry shirts returning from wherever. The Calabrian mix makes for a rich temperament. In addition to the Greek philosophers and poets, there were the persecuted Protestant Valdesians of Val d'Aosta who found haven here, and the Albanian anarchists who, as political exiles, formed permanent colonies in different areas of Calabria and gave rise to the saying, "If one meets a wolf and an Albanian in the forest, shoot first at the Albanian."

But let me return to Castagna, for it's really there, almost equidistant inland from the Ionian Sea on the east and the Tyrrhenian Sea on the west. The nearest cities are Cosenza or Catanzaro in whose province it lies, but these places are almost as remote to the villagers as Rome or Naples. Castagna's market town is Soveria Mannelli, twelve kilometers away on the provincial paved roadway. On the principal street of Soveria Mannelli a plaque records that Giuseppe Garibaldi, Cavalier of Humanity and Hero of the Most High Order, on his way to unite Italy, there spent the night of August 30, 1860. The Bourbons surrendered en masse at his approach, and of his bloodless passage there remain as memorials the fourth-class Hotel Garibaldi with accommodations for eleven, and an obelisk in the piazza around which the outdoor market spreads itself.

Also on that main street of Soveria Mannelli I saw a sign announcing *Articoli di Regalo*, gift items, and watch repairs, followed by the owner's name, A. Cardamone, which might have been the same as my grandfather's. It was midday, the shop was closed, so I could not meet the proprietor and possible kinsperson. I found two other family names in the telephone directory listed for Soveria Mannelli and none for Castagna because there is only one telephone in the village and it belongs to the Salt and Tobacco shop. In Cosenza there were seven names, one identified as a fruit vendor and another as a professor. The name derives either from an Eastern spice plant called *kardamon* in Greek or from one who cards wool, and, if this last, in Italian one who is a carder is a tease (a "card?") and, worse, a backbiter. This meaning derives from the Latin *cardus*, thistle, whose prickles were used to card wool; then, figuratively, the meaning extends to include the prickles of a verbal barb, as in bad-mouthing. Which might account for some of the American Cardamone women to whom I am related.

A few miles out of Soveria Manelli, a dirt road turns off the paved one and traverses a valley through which runs the small river called Corace. Castagna came in sight on a prospect among chestnut, beech, and pine trees overlooking the valley where are found the ruins of the Norman abbey. It was a totally romantic and unexpected sight to find those ivy-covered walls with tufts of flowering growth sprouting out of crevices; it would not have been out of place in England.

I could never imagine that my grandparents had such sights in their daily lives, for my mother, who had spent only that appalling night in a dark loft in the village, never got to see the valley below and so tell us about it—she and my father fled as soon as it was light without a glance around them. When I arrived, the air was moving and fresh; shadows of dark green growth cut the heat of the hot sun. The little stream had real running water, was not one of those dry riverbeds that are called *torrente* but have at best a modest torrent in the spring and lie empty most of the year as ruts in the treeless plains. Big light green burrs shone from the darker leaves of the chestnut trees. I was glad that the valley and its abbey were part of Castagna's purview and that I had some connection with that very spot in all the world.

At the entrance to the village, Niki got out and took a drink from a fountain that ran cool, fresh water into a basin. Did the village women still collect it in jars? As I watched Niki I wondered, did the water come from the mountain spring where her name-sake had drunk as a goat-girl? Water as refresher, restorer was becoming part of the story that was forming in me.

Nobody was about; a scruffy old woman stuck her head out a window—she bore a marked resemblance in deshabille to that dignified matron of Utica, New York, Mrs. Jim Scala, my mother's godmother, whose people were also from Castagna; some little boys hopped about for attention. But the place was mostly quiet—there wasn't even the scratching of chickens. There was nothing in Castagna except for the postal room with a stopped clock on the wall, a tiny, dark bar, and the *Sale e Tabacchi* store where the only phone in the village could be used at the posted times: weekdays, 8:00–12:00 and 14:00–19:00, and holidays, 9:00–12:00.

There was nothing left to do but call on the parish priest, who turned out to be a northerner from Livorno. Meeting him, I felt like Gissing, who, when he once came to a bleaker-than-usual town, had asked, "What do people do here?" only to be answered, "*C'è la miseria.*"

"Where are the people?" I asked the priest.

"They've all gone," he said; "first to America, now to Germany or Milan, Turin." When he first arrived, three years before, there were supposed to have been twelve hundred souls in Castagna for him to tend, but it was more like eight hundred. Now it was half that, mostly women and children whose men had gone elsewhere to work.

The place was poor; there were no stores, no eating places, no cultivated fields, nothing but chestnuts which the remaining people gathered. But it was clean, and the children didn't run after us with sorrowful eyes, begging. The little streets were not the seamy alleys of Palermo or Naples. Some of the homes, poor stone dwellings which had been shaken by earth tremors, were propped up by thick tree limbs, but there was no squalor or filth. Still, one knew why the people of Castagna had left.

When my grandmother died I was a child; it took thirty-seven years for me to get to her grave in Utica. It was a going back, reascending time to the places of my youth and to an awareness of where the end of my own journey will be. Death is now something to think of. Not morbidly, but with recognition, acknowledging a part of life that hadn't, before Antonio's death, occupied me. Before, there were other matters: children, schooling, moving, home life, work. But it all goes so quickly. He died suddenly just after the first of our girls left for college in the States. He had been very fond of Croton-on-Hudson when we lived there and used to say of the old burying ground on the hill, "This is where I will be buried." But he died suddenly in Rome, and the dignitaries of Vicenza asked that he be buried there, in his birthplace, in a part of the cemetery set aside for its honored sons. Antonio is there with another poet, Giacomo Zanella, some other writers, artists, jurists, scholars, as well as Count Giuseppe Rossi, who founded the town's wool industry; and nearby are Antonio's mother, father, and sister. He is home, but it left me wondering where I'd eventually be.

I live in the river town of Hastings-on-Hudson. Two daughters are nearby while another has long returned to marry and live in Italy; and so it will always be—some here, some there, just as we were always journeying between America and Italy and in a figurative sense always will be.

On a last trip back to Syracuse to see my parents, some pieces of this puzzle I've been working at, off and on, for half a century, came into place: I began to see a circle completing. My parents were still members of the Yacht Club, and we drove out there during my visit. I walked down to the lakeshore where I had swum as a child. It is even more desolate now than then, for no attempt at a sandy beach is made any longer and the old dock is gone, sunken or taken down; now the members' children swim in a pool of chlorinated water put into what used to be a fine lawn sweeping down to the boat harbor from the club veranda. Grey and somber as it is, I prefer the lake and its view toward the islands. And as I stood on the shore, Frenchman's Island beckoned the same as ever. I no longer think of swimming there—that project has passed into mythology. I simply know now what I didn't know then, that Alexis de Tocqueville had once come to Lake Oneida, not by mere chance, but as the fulfillment of a real desire from his boyhood in France to get to Frenchman's Island in the New World.

Tocqueville visited the United States as a young man and on July 7, 1831, he set out from Syracuse with a companion. They went on horseback through "immense forest" to Fort Brewerton, where they caught their first glimpse of Oneida Lake—then, as now, silent, grey, lonely, brooding.

Years before, Tocqueville had been stirred by the story of a young Frenchman and his wife who, driven from their country by the Revolution, had come to the New World and taken refuge on an island in Lake Oneida. There, cut off from the whole world, far from the storms of Europe and the society into which they had been born, the two outcasts lived for one another and found peace in their solitary haven. (This reminded me of the time when, during an intermission of the contemporary opera *Ghosts of Versailles*, I overheard the improbable comment that Marie Antoinette was supposed to have been wafted off to safety in the New World, either to Philadelphia or to Frenchman's Island in upstate New York where a two-story log cabin awaited her.)

To Tocqueville, the island must have seemed a kind of Eden, for it became a saying of his that "the only happiness in the world is on the shores of Lake Oneida."

At South Bay he and his companion stopped at a hut on the lakeshore occupied by a fisherman's wife who said, yes, the larger of the two islands was named for the Frenchman who had lived there at one time, but when she herself had visited the island some time ago, it was already deserted and she had seen the remains of a dwelling in the midst of cleared land where some fruits and flowers still grew. The Frenchman had left the island after his wife died and no one had inhabited it since.

Tocqueville and his friend rowed out to the island, and beyond the belt of huge and ancient trees nearest the shore they found younger growth taking over land that they could see had once been cleared. They searched awhile before they found an old apple tree and a once-cultivated vine, now gone wild, climbing the trees of the encroaching woods; by scooping away the thick bed of leaves on the ground, they were able to make out some debris of the rude cabin that had stood there and so speculate on the fate that had touched their compatriots decades before. They carved their names on a tree, Tocqueville said, and sadly left, reflecting on fate and the circumstances which sweep men hither and yon, from one land to another.

He, European, had searched for the touch of man's hand on the wilderness; he was moved by human emotions; and yet he felt a sense of conflict, of contradiction when faced by the majesty of nature pure: "One feels proud to be a man," he wrote, "and yet at the same time one experiences I cannot say what bitter regret at the power God has granted us over nature. One's soul is shaken by contradictory thoughts and feelings."

No matter how much reverence he felt for the forest's majesty, Tocqueville, supremely civilized and humanized as he was, felt also the need to discern the imprint of man that subdues the forest primeval and offers, in the stead of blind thickets, the principles of that reasoned cultivation which is balance—the classical attitude.

And I remembered, so long after Tocqueville, how my own European husband had stood with my father on the shore of Oneida Lake and had had a sense of wilderness as he looked across the gray, remorseless water embellished only with the green of the two islands. He was filled with more than nostalgia for the Old World; he felt awe, too, for all those faced with the toughness, the grittiness of the New—awe for the Frenchman who had come and set up a home on that island.

"This is Lake Oneida," my father had said to Antonio, "this is our Lake Como. We have the best pike in the world from this lake."

Antonio admired my father, and felt, he told me, his gallantry in boasting of his world. At the same time Antonio also felt as if in Syracuse he were already in the heart of an immense continent. There was such a sense of being inland, far from the sea, in a land still untamed and wild and unused to man, that it was almost palpable to him, he who was used to the gentle hills of Vicenza with their well-tended fields and signs of millennia of cultivation and human touch upon them. He missed the sense of order an old culture transmitted, the needed corrective to what is disordered, random. His real feeling of restiveness was for those pockets of civilization that had the feeling of being encircled by a wilderness waiting always to take over. Oneida was not Lake Como, nor are there now pike (or any fish) to be taken from its polluted waters.

Nature, in Italy, is tamed, cultivated as in the rules set down by Vergil in his *Georgics* or in the bucolics of Theocritus, the Greek poet of ancient Syracuse. Now that I have lived in Italy, I know there is something indomitable and wild in the American landscape even in this built-up East where my home is now. There is still a sense of forest even in my small-town garden if I don't relentlessly prune, weed, and pull out the envois of latent thickets.

I know those feelings of contradictories of which Tocqueville spoke—the search for balance and order cohabiting with the deep certainty that all will change and pass no matter what order is imposed. Thus wilderness reclaimed the Frenchman's island orchard and vines; and thus, Kroton, whose ancient people were so noted for their beauty and athletic prowess that "healthier than Kroton" had been the hyperbole of antiquity to measure anything fabulous, had become by Gissing's day a malarial pesthole of deformed and ugly creatures. Even as we transform, we must still maintain our island of order in this life.

It comes down to a question of balance—to avoid both the Calabrian desolation that came with too much of man's taking over nature and felling the forests, or total engulfment by a senseless nature; to strike a balance between excesses of any kind, between too European or too American a way. Balance seemed what classicism was all about, and that, I reflected on the banks of Oneida Lake, was perhaps what I had been striving for without knowing it when I yearned to swim to Frenchman's Island.

But let me not pretend too much. Let me not say that I had articulated such thoughts or even felt some special sense of destiny connected with that island. That, no; but its allure and mystery, yes. For the name alone, exotic in itself, was bound to have spoken to my age and condition at that time.

Now I can read into the past all sorts of formerly illegible messages (as if they had been written in an invisible ink that comes to sight only when a flame is passed over it, or on a palimpsest finally scraped down to the original notation). Now I can almost believe I once did pass by Tocqueville's name scratched on a tree at Frenchman's Island like a signal to me to seek the Old World in order to achieve balance with the New. And so I could now almost allegorize the whole idea of the swim to Frenchman's Island. But no, that would impose too much on this story, and besides it's not true, only a passing thought.

During that same visit to my parents in Syracuse, we drove to Utica, where my mother had grown up. We went back to see the old Queen Anne house at 722 Rutger Street she had lived in. It's still there, well kept and comfortable looking. Then we visited the cemetery.

The family plot is on the highest point of Calvary Cemetery, identified by a large wooden cross that gives the cemetery its name. It is a large plot, enough for twenty-four graves; though not nearly large enough for all the descendants of my Utica grandparents, it will still probably never be filled, for most of their family have left for other places. A large stone angel, for Grandfather Angelo whom I never knew, tops the substantial tombstone engraved with the family name. There he lies along with his wife Nicoletta, the silent old woman in black who managed, somehow, to tell me volumes.

They lie in the middle of a green expanse on top of a pleasant hill, with trees and bushes, that looks down over Utica where they settled; and I am glad they are on a hill with trees, even though they are maples and not the huge chestnuts of Castagna. Before them, in a front row of low markers, are the children who preceded them: a daughter named Rosina who died at twelve of what was then called galloping tuberculosis, and three grandchildren, cousins of mine, who died in their youth. Flanking the large tombstone are the markers of the two eldest sons, my mother's brothers, and their wives. Also there, without a spouse, is my mother's oldest sister, Aunt Cora, who had been deserted years before by her husband. My other aunts were laid to rest with their husbands in separate family plots.

It was not a sad occasion, that cemetery visit; it was touching and beautiful to find so many of the family together, to see the names marked on the stones and to remember the persons they evoked. There was moon-faced Uncle Frank who was always smiling and calling out to us, "You fresh kids!" There was dour Uncle Sam, who looked so much like my grandmother, and his only son called Spike who used to wear knickerbockers and play the mandolin at family picnics. There was my young cousin Tony, a handsome boy known for his high dives and twists who died suddenly at only seventeen. And there was Aunt Mary, who had once had a beautiful white collie dog named Duchess and a house that was wonderful to play in.

It was a serene visit; it brought them all back to mind. Most moving of all was Aunt Cora, not alone in death as she had been in life, but back with her family. I think it was in that moment that I wondered where I would finally rest, and it came to me that, wherever it was, it could not be with Antonio, for he was interred with his fellow honored citizens of Vicenza and there was no place there for me. Death suddenly seemed lonely, for I would be in a solitary grave with no one near of the same name.

Then I wondered if my parents had a family plot, for in all such matters—planning future security, having things done on time, looking ahead, acting responsibly—my father had exerted his greatest efforts. I was astounded at what my mother told me: he was almost eighty and hadn't gotten around to buying a cemetery plot.

"When you do," I told him that night, "get space for three. I'll come wherever you and Mother will be."

They were surprised; my daughters were surprised; I was surprised. But my feeling was genuine. I did not want to rest alone in the cemetery of a place where I just happened to be living. Since I could not have a family plot with Antonio, why not go back to Syracuse, my circular journey ending in St. Mary's Cemetery not far from my brothers' homes. Then, when their children and mine come to visit and remember their grandparents, they will be visiting me, too.

And on my stone will be carved those lines from his *Ode to Catullus* that the poet had read aloud to me not long after we first met in Florence:

> *ora la fanciulla è sogno,*
> *sogno il poeta e l'amore.*

Now the girl is a dream / a dream the poet and love.